Discover
G.O.D.
GOD'S ORIGINAL DESIGN
for YOUth

No longer a slave to labels of man

by Sheri Yates

Publisher iKAN Publish
iKANPublish.com

Discover G.O.D. God's "Original Design" for Youth
By Sheri Yates

We would love to hear from you.
God's Original Design Youth Group
www.ikanministries.com

Copyright © 2015 by Sheri Yates

Unless otherwise noted, Scripture quotations are taken from the Holy Bible, New International Version. Copyright © 1973, 1978, 1984 by the International Bible Society. Used by permission of the International Bible Society.

Scripture quotations marked (AMP) are taken from the Amplified® Bible. Copyright © 1954, 1958, 1962, 1964, 1965, 1987 by The Lockman Foundation. Used by permission." (www.Lockman.org)

Scripture quotations marked (ESV) are taken from The Holy Bible, English Standard Version (ESV), copyright © 2001 by Crossway Bibles, a publishing ministry of Good News Publishers. Used by permission. All rights reserved.

ISBN-13:978-1517166113
ISBN-10:151716611X

Cover and Interior Design: iPublicidades.com
Cover Artwork: Spencer Lauren Yates
Confession Writing: Josh Pugh
Interior Drawings: Katie Candle Moore and Spencer Lauren Yates
Interior Word Art and Interior Image: Chandler Yates
Editor and Dreamstormer: Kathleen Ray Hildenbrand
Wordsmith: Kathleen Ray Hildenbrand
Technical Writing: Adam Swiger
Organizer and Sheri's Right-Hand: Nona Cruz

Printed in the United States of America

FOREWORD

Everyone was created with a purpose in the world—an original design. This book is written with the motivation of assisting young people in knowing themselves, knowing God, and knowing themselves in God. This is the Original Design.

The book introduces God, His love, and Truth as a trustworthy source of identity. It discusses His intended purpose for everyone. Assignments and activities are provided to facilitate practice for the new work that has been delegated along with this identity.

This is simply an all-around workbook for young believers pursuing their Truth in Jesus.

INTRODUCTION

Your view of God will determine whether you are victorious or smashed under the weight of a trial. This book is designed for youth to know and fall totally in love with God as they encounter the person of Jesus. It builds the foundation and identity of each young adult. The impact is a long arm reaching out into a broken world with the love of God as these youth are released to practice their faith in real life scenarios.

Our prayer is that you will encounter the love of God like never before and stand on your own firm foundation, not your parents, friends, pastors and that your own footing is deeply rooted and mightily established in the Word and in God's radical love.

Each week, we will renew our strength in learning to be still and listening to God's voice. We are His sheep. We hear His voice, but we only need to be still. We believe in you! We believe that with our support, you will have the opportunity to experience God more.

As our roots are becoming established, we will labor in our faith. We will attempt hometown missionary trips, pray over parents, and invite the community in for prayer and worship as we learn to hear from the Lord and speak His encouragements over our community.

We pray that your entire family will be blessed in this season as the youth pursue God with everything – whole heart, mind, strength, and soul.

DEDICATION

Thank you to all the leaders of God's Original Design at ikanministries.com for loving God and these young adults more than imaginable! Thank you for your faithfulness, for finding time to build community, for worshipping God with music, time, gifts, and talents. Mostly, thank you for loving Jesus and for choosing unity, life, and the narrow path.

Thank you to the Original Design Youth Group for pursuing God more than anything. You hunger for Him! You love Him. You desperately seek Him. You honor Him with your friendships. You pursue righteousness. You pursue Truth! You are a world changer. We believe in you!

> *"I don't believe God's called me to survive the world but to change it for His glory."*
> — STEVEN FURTICK

NOTE FROM SHERI

It is amazing how God led the hearts of those involved in our ministry to drastically change the direction of our Youth! We are redefining fun! Fun is not playing games to no end. Fun is fully knowing God and seeing His power in THIS life!

As we dreamed together, we could see the potential of what God could do with this kind of focus and dedication. It wasn't until I heard the song, Still

Believe by Kim Walker-Smith that God gave me a vision for this book! I got it on a Friday and had finished writing this book on Monday! No joke! When God gives you a vision, He gives you what you need to complete it. Sure it took my time, but it was not a burdensome task. It was like pouring water out of pitcher! I was ready to pour out what God had already been speaking to my heart for the past six months!

I praise God for this work! I am thankful to be His hands and feet and for Kathleen dreaming this up with me! Many distractions will try to take you out of God's will. The enemy will throw many darts until he finds the one that will take you away from what you are called to do by God. Don't fall for any of them! Keep your eyes ahead. Don't turn to the right or the left. Ever.

NOTE FROM KATHLEEN

This book is a miracle! We have kicked this idea around for years, but it turned out so much more than we have ever imagined. The vision that God gave Sheri was incredible! A fierce example of how when you ask the Lord gives. What a privilege to see this come to life and so quickly! We will always be able to look back and remember what God did!

You are fully known and loved by God. Imagine what our families, better yet, this world would be like if everyone knew this simple Truth. We pray that even as you touch this book you will be fully healed, restored, set free, and brought back into the fullness of all of God's promises!

We know that lives will be transformed and that millions will be impacted because we have prayed and fully believe that the Father's love will ignite each reader to share God's far-reaching love everyday with the world around them.

TABLE OF CONTENTS

Encounter Love 17

Who Do You Say That I Am 21

You are Fully Known and Loved 25

Fun is…Bringing Heaven to Earth 33

You Do Hear His Voice 37

I Am 41

Jesus Is The I Am 47

When Jesus Declared "I AM" 53

Your Original Design - IDNJC 55

Do You Know How You Move God? 61

The Original Design of Others 67

Idol Worship 73

Is God Your First 77

Worship is a Response 81

Super Power to Witness 85

Do You Want a Super Power 91

Secret Language 97

Forgive Quickly 103

Work With Others – Not alone 107

Great Commission Practice Round 111
Delegated Authority 117
Hometown Missionary 121
Speak to Your Mountain 127
Resist the Devil 133
Take Possession 137
Armed in Attitude 143
Greater Things 145
The Great Commission 151
Keep It Simple – Share Your Story 155
Faith Without Works is DEAD 159

APPENDIX

When Jesus Didn't Do Miracles 165
Your Sword 169

CONFESSIONS

IDNJC 173
Where is My God? 175
Religion 177
God Changes Me 179
Who I Am In Christ 180
What Am I? 183
Mind of Christ 185

Table of Contents

LEADER PRACTICE OPPORTUNITIES

One Word 189

Speak A Blessing 190

Hometown Missionary Form 191

Listening 193

Speak Life 194

Search For Jesus in Others 195

Serve 196

Wash Feet 197

Original Design Prayer 199

OTHER

Doodles and Notes 201

Acknowledgements 209

About the Book, Author, and Director of G.O.D 213

GOD is LOVE

LET'S ENCOUNTER HIS LOVE NOW!

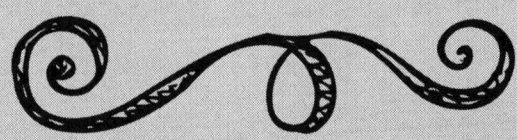

"EVERY HEART WAS MADE FOR LOVE, CREATED IN THE IMAGE OF LOVE HIMSELF."

— Misty Edwards

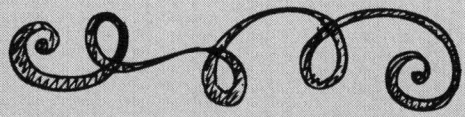

ENCOUNTER LOVE

I think many people are desperate for an encounter with God. What if you could be the encounter they desperately need? Did you know that you carry the love of God everywhere? Maybe YOU need an encounter with God's love. If so, ask God for one. He lavishes His love on you. He loves you so much. Hold onto and cherish everything God has already done for you to keep your love for Him alive and fresh.

Look up these verses to discover how loved by God you truly are.

Jeremiah 1:5
Ephesians 1:4
Romans 5:8
James 1:17-18
John 3:16-17

> *Review the following chart. Circle all the attributes of God that you experience now. SQUARE the ones you want to experience.*

"Listen, O daughter,
consider & give ear:

FORGET your people &
your FATHER'S HOUSE.

The KING is enthralled
by your BEAUTY;

HONOR him,
for he is your Lord.

Here is a list of some of God's names. How would you like to experience Him this year? Square them. Ask Him. As you grow throughout the year, refer back to this.

MOST HIGH GOD	KING OF KINGS	PROTECTOR
DELIVERER	JESUS! LAMB OF GOD	OMNISCIENT
FORTRESS		TRUTH
CREATOR	EVERLASTING GOD	NAME ABOVE ALL NAMES
I AM!	LOVE	
ABBA FATHER	LIVING WATER	NEAR
THE LORD MY BANNER	SHEPHERD	EQUIPPER
	COMFORTER	HOLY
ALL-KNOWING	PROTECTED	GOOD
ABUNDANT	HEALER	PRINCE OF PEACE
PROVIDER	DWELLING PLACE	RIGHTEOUS
ABOVE ALL	FRIEND	MERCIFUL
BEGINNING	MASTER	FAITHFUL
RESTORER	REDEEMER	UNCHANGING
BRIDEGROOM	TEACHER	OMNIPOTENT
BREAD OF LIFE	ALL-SUFFICIENT ONE	OMNIPRESENT
THE LORD OF LORDS	SHEPHERD	SOVEREIGN
JUST	WAY	PURSUER
IMMANUEL	SAVIOR	

This is a short list of the character of God. He has many more names than this! As He reveals Himself to you in new ways, add the names to this list.

WHO DO YOU SAY THAT I AM

I was prompted years ago to listen to a song and circle how I was experiencing God at that moment. What I didn't know is that my mom would be diagnosed with cancer and I would spend over half of the next year in a hospital. Also at that time, I didn't know that I would be a mom again. A year later, I listened to this song again and circled how I was experiencing God at that time.

I looked down at the list and wept because who God was to me between the 12 months had COMPLETELY changed. I was experiencing my Father God differently – like I had never before.

Jesus asked His disciples, "Who do you say that I am?"

Now I am asking you, who do you say God is?

GREG FERGUSON – PEACE MAKER LYRICS

Peacemaker, Fear Taker, Soul Soother, Storm Smoother
Light Shiner, Lost Finder, Cloud Lifter, Deliverer,
Heart Toucher, Truth Lover,
Who other could be Fear Taker, Peacemaker

Mind Clearer, Sigh Healer, Hand Holder, Counselor,
Wound Binder, Tear Dryer, Strength Giver, Provider,
Heart Healer, Kind Father,

Who other could be, My Savior, Peacemaker
Let Your Peace Rule in my heart,
Let Your kindness fill my thoughts,
Let Your strength secure my soul,
Let Your peace take hold in me,
Let Your Wisdom guide my will,
Your compassion fill this place,
Let my anxious thoughts be still,

Let Your peace rule in my Heart.

Circle WHO God is to you TODAY. Write down the date so you can refer back to it.

Date: _____

YOU ARE FULLY KNOWN AND LOVED

What are you looking for? Why are you searching out the love of a girlfriend or boyfriend? Why are you trying so hard to earn the love of friends that if you're totally honest, you do not necessarily like them? It's impossible to truly love someone else until you are fully secure in God's love for you and you love yourself. There is a reason why the 2nd greatest command is to "love others as yourself!" It implies that you ALREADY love yourself!

TBH, we all desperately long to be fully known, loved, cherished, pursued by someone – anyone really! Admit it, don't we strive to fit in so that maybe…just maybe…someone will pay attention to us – and eventually love us. That's why we try to find the approval of our parents sometimes to the point of keeping secrets because you don't want them to know your real struggles because you're afraid of losing their love. Some of us will do most about anything to gain the attention of our parents – some may think that negative attention is better than no attention. My, Sheri, little sister once said, "I would rather have negative attention than no attention.

Do you fully LOVE yourself? I mean truly love – as in, do you love every perceived flaw? Or do you compare yourself to others and desperately wish you could have their hair, nose, popularity, personality, hunting skills, parents, car, _____, _____, _____, _____, _____, _____whatever. You list your things.

Guess what? You are already fully known and loved by God! You cannot earn His love. He will never withdraw it from you!

> *Are you secure in His love for you today?*
>
> *Read Psalm 139 and Romans 8:38-39.*

God knows you! God loves you! He longs to be loved and known by you.

> *Let these verses SINK Deep within you. Let them renew your mind fully! Stopped trying to get what you already have! Receive His Love tonight. Write down your favorite verse.*

GOD,

the Creator of the Universe,

LOVES YOU.

yes, you.

Let that sink in.

"HOW HE LOVES"
by Jesus Culture

He is jealous for me
Love's like a hurricane, and I am a tree
Bending beneath the weight of His wind and mercy
When all of a sudden,
I am unaware of these afflictions eclipsed by glory
And I realize just how beautiful you are and how great your affections are for me.

How He loves us
He loves us
His presence. His love.
Is so thick and tangible in this room tonight.
And there are some of you here that have not encountered the love of God.
And tonight God wants to encounter you.
And wants you to feel His love.
His amazing love.
Without it these are just songs.
These are just words.
These are just instruments.
Without the love of God, it's just like we're just up here just making noise.
But the love of God changes us,
And we're never the same,
We're never the same
After we encounter the love of God
We're never the same after we encounter the love of God
And right now if you haven't encountered the love of God,
And you would know,
Because you wouldn't be the same.

You would never be the same again.
And if you, if you, want to encounter the love of
God right now,
You better just brace yourself because He's about to
just blow in this place
And we're gonna encounter the love of God right now.
So God I speak to all the hearts
And I ask God that every heart be open right now
Every heart be open.
Every spirit be opened up
To you God. To You.
And a love encounter
A love encounter from you tonight
A love encounter from you tonight God.

Yeah He loves us
Oh how He loves us
Oh how He loves
Let it go deep go deep go deep

We are His portion and He is our prize
Drawn to redemption by the grace in his eyes
If grace is an ocean, we're all sinking (ha ha)
So heaven meets earth like a sloppy wet kiss
And my heart turns violently inside of my chest
I don't have time to maintain these regrets
when I think about the way

He loves us
Oh how he loves us
oh how he loves us
oh how he loves

YOU ARE FULLY KNOWN AND LOVED

His love is going deep
His love is going deep tonight
His love is going deep tonight
See the Father
Behold the Father
Behold the Father

FUN IS...BRINGING HEAVEN TO EARTH

Jesus prayed this prayer, "Your Kingdom come, Your will be done, on earth as it is in Heaven" before He was crucified. I believe that as Jesus walked on the earth, he did bring heaven to earth. He healed whole crowds, fed the multitudes, set people free, and much more. You have the opportunity to read about His works in the Greater Things chapter. People followed Him because He changed their life, He lavished love on them with the power of God, and they wanted what He had. I bet they never wanted to leave His presence so that's why many asked if they could become a disciple too.

I believe when people encountered Him, they ran into freedom, whole-ness, healing, and love. This is fun. Fun isn't playing video games to no end! Fun is seeing God's miracles on this earth!

THE LORD'S PRAYER

Our Father in heaven,
hallowed be your name,
your kingdom come,
your will be done,
on earth as in heaven.
Give us today our daily bread.
Forgive us our sins
as we forgive those who sin against us.
Lead us not into temptation
but deliver us from evil.
For the kingdom, the power,
and the glory are yours
now and for ever.
Amen.

> *We are called to bring heaven to earth by being the hands and feet of Jesus – loving the unlovable and speaking to mountains and seeing them retract! BOOM!*
>
> *Write down what fun, entertaining thing that has entrapped you. What would you like to give up so that you can seek God more and be His hands and feet?*

"YOU DON'T HAVE TO KNOW WHAT TO SAY OR WHAT TO DO; JUST LISTEN TO THE ONE WHO SENT YOU."

— Craig Groeschel

YOU DO HEAR HIS VOICE

Can you hear God's voice? Maybe you are not sure, if you hear yourself asking: "Is this God or is this me?"

Distractions! I can barely hear myself think! Distractions divide our attention…right?! It's hard to study for school and pet our horse at the same time. It's impossible to read Shakespeare and hunt, right? It's hard to read the Bible while texting friends.

Maybe you are a person who is a skilled listener, or—like me—maybe you are the one who never stops talking long enough to listen.

Are you busy, distracted, talking, or figuring out what to say so you can look cool to your squad or simply fit it? There are so many pressures to stay popular. Truth is…you cannot possibly listen and truly hear simultaneously. And all those friends you are working so hard to impress, really need a friend that will listen whom they can trust!

The same is true when we are trying to hear from the Lord. He is gentle and kind. To hear Him, we need to learn HOW to listen.

It starts with being still. For you, are you only still while sleeping? That is not what I mean here. Let us turn that around and learn to be still and that will result in becoming an excellent listener.

The best, long-term friendships I, Sheri, have are the ones that we can be fully ourselves with no masks. We give and take the praiseworthy, good, bad, and ugly. We can easily talk for hours and plunge into deep conversations, trust each other implicitly, can count on one another regardless of the circumstance, and honestly – it's fun!

Learning to listen will help you know and love God's friendship more. As you become more intimate with Him, you are able to surrender your guarded heart so that you can love others more!

> "To be a Christian without prayer is no more possible than to be alive without breathing."
> — MARTIN LUTHER KING JR.

1. Write down how you know the difference between God's voice and your head voice.

2. Have you heard from God before? If so, when and what did you hear? Many people say, "In the shower." Why? Because in the shower we are still and there are no other distractions.

The Bible is FULL of words God has ALREADY spoken to you. If you really want to hear Him and know Him, consume the BIBLE! Read it day and night! He will speak to you through it.

Besides, if you don't know the Bible (God's voice), then when you do hear something, how will you know if it's God or the enemy? God never lies and He voice always aligns with THE WORD – BIBLE.

> *Look up and read John 10. Compile a list of character traits revealed in these verses. Do you see any of these? Others?*
>
> *Add to this list.*

Names and Character of God	Verse
Calls you by name	3
Full Life	10
Gat	7
Goes ahead of you	4
Good Shepherd	2

I
AM

I AM

I AM are two of the most powerful words ever spoken.

When you hear yourself speaking about who you are, what do you hear? Circle and add to the list what you have said about yourself the past month.

I AM:

Fat	*Worthless*	*Insecure*
Stupid	*Sarcastic*	*Popular*
Secure	*Kind*	*Generous*
Loud	*Rejected*	*Insignificant*
Dingy	*Life of the Party*	*Idiot*
Funny	*Purposeless*	*Desperate*
Helpless	*Awkward*	*Beautiful*
Boring	*Weird*	*Unpopular*
Loving	*Jealous*	*3rd Wheel*
Fun	*Annoying*	*Loner*
Friendless	*No one likes me*	*Ungifted*
Afraid	*Quiet*	*Unqualified*
Ugly	*Shy*	*Excluded*

Out of your mouth, you speak life or death – Proverbs 18:21. Stop right now speaking death over yourself! Speak Life! Turn it up! Look at HOW POWERFUL I AM is in the following verses.

Holy, holy, holy **is** the Lord God Almighty, who was, and is, AND is To Come.

God told Moses who he was. He said "I AM." It means that I Am That I Am. It means He is all in all. He lacks nothing. He is complete. He is the beginning and the end. He is. Read Exodus 3:14

Matthew Henry Commentary says this about I AM.

> "God would now be known by a name that denotes what he is in himself, I AM THAT I AM. This explains his name Jehovah, and signifies, 1. That he is self-existent: he has his being of himself. 2. That he is eternal and unchangeable, and always the same, yesterday, today, and forever. 3. That he is incomprehensible; we cannot by searching find him out: this name checks all bold and curious inquiries concerning God. 4. That he is faithful and true to all his promises, unchangeable in his word as well as in his nature; let Israel know this, I AM hath sent me unto you. I am, and there is none else besides me. All else have their being from God, and are wholly dependent upon him."

Check out all the times God said, "I AM."

"I AM," STATEMENTS OF GOD

Genesis 15:1, "I am your shield; your reward shall be very great."

Genesis 15:7, "I am the Lord who brought you out from Ur of the Chaldeans to give you this land to possess."

Genesis 17:1-2, "I am God Almighty; walk before me, and be blameless, that I may make my covenant between me and you, and may multiply you greatly."

Genesis 26:24, "I am the God of Abraham your father. Fear not, for I am with you and will bless you and multiply your offspring for my servant Abraham's sake."

Genesis 35:11, "I am God Almighty: be fruitful and multiply. A nation and a company of nations shall come from you, and kings shall come from your own body."

Genesis 46:3, "I am God, the God of your father. Do not be afraid to go down to Egypt, for there I will make you into a great nation."

Exodus 3:6, "And he said, "I am the God of your father, the God of Abraham, the God of Isaac, and the God of Jacob." And Moses hid his face, for he was afraid to look at God.

Exodus 3:14, "God said to Moses, "I am who I am." And he said, "Say this to the people of Israel, 'I am has sent me to you.'"

Exodus 6:2, "God spoke to Moses and said to him, 'I am the Lord.'"

Exodus 16:12, "I have heard the grumbling of the people of Israel. Say to them, 'At twilight you shall eat meat, and in the morning you shall be filled with bread.' Then you shall know that I am the Lord your God."

Exodus 20:2, "I am the Lord your God, who brought you out of the land of Egypt, out of the house of slavery."

Exodus 29:34, "And they shall know that I am the Lord their God, who brought them out of the land of Egypt that I might dwell among them. I am the Lord their God."

Deuteronomy 5:6, "I am the Lord your God, who brought you out of the land of Egypt, out of the house of slavery."

Deuteronomy 29:5-6, "I have led you forty years in the wilderness. Your clothes have not worn out on you, and your sandals have not worn off your feet. You have not eaten bread, and you have not drunk wine or strong drink, that you may know that I am the LORD your God."

Deuteronomy 32:39, "See now that I, even I, am he, and there is no god beside me; I kill and I make alive; I wound and I heal; and there is none that can deliver out of my hand."

Isaiah 43:13, "Also henceforth I am he; there is none who can deliver from my hand; I work, and who can turn it back?"

Isaiah 43:25, "I, even I, am he who blots out your transgressions for my own sake, and I will not remember your sins."

Isaiah 46:3-4, "Listen to me, O house of Jacob, all the remnant of the house of Israel, who have been borne by me from before your birth, carried from the womb; even to your old age I am he, and to gray hairs I will carry you. I have made, and I will bear; I will carry and will save."

Isaiah 48:12, "Listen to me, O Jacob, and Israel, whom I called! I am he; I am the first, and I am the last.

Isaiah 51:12, "I, even I, am he who comforts you."

Isaiah 52:6, "Therefore my people shall know my name. Therefore in that day they shall know that it is I who speak; here I am."

Source: http://rj-mccauley.blogspot.com/2013/03/the-i-am-of-old-testament-in-new.html

> *When we refer to ourselves as "I am…." and pair it with some negative and demeaning self-slander, we misunderstand the power in this these words we speak. How do you replace your trash talk with God's truth?*

Doodle Page

JESUS IS THE I AM

Young Men – you will love this. Jesus knocked over an entire army with His words! Look at how powerful the words "I AM" are when Jesus said it!

JOHN 18:4-6 AMPLIFIED BIBLE (AMP)

4 Then Jesus, knowing all that was about to befall Him, went out to them and said, Whom are you seeking? [Whom do you want?] 5 They answered Him, Jesus the Nazarene. Jesus said to them, I am He. Judas, who was betraying Him, was also standing with them. 6 When Jesus said to them, I am He, they went backwards (drew back, lurched backward) and fell to the ground.

Now, the Bible says that you have the Holy Spirit, which is Jesus' Spirit. If the same power of Jesus lives within you, than "I AM" should be two of the most powerful words you speak also! The "I AM" statements you speak over yourself are either killing you or healing you!

> *"If you want to change the direction of your life, change the declaration of your lips."*
> — STEVEN FURTICK

Who God says you are is your Original Design! Stop trying to become who you already are. You must look through God's eyes to see yourself completely!

> *Circle the ones you KNOW you are. SQUARE the ones you struggle with believing.*

I am God's possession. (Gen. 17:8; 1 Cor. 6:20)
I am God's child. (John 1:12)
I am God's workmanship. (Eph. 2:10)
I am God's friend. (James 2:23)
I am God's temple. (1 Cor. 3:16, 6:16)
I am God's vessel. (2 Tim. 2:2)
I am God's laborer. (1 Tim. 5:18)
I am God's witness. (Acts 1:8)
I am God's soldier. (2 Tim. 2:3)
I am God's ambassador. (2 Cor. 5:20)
I am God's building. (1 Cor. 3:9)
I am God's chosen. (Eph. 1:4)
I am God's beloved. (Rom. 1:7; 2 Thess. 2:13)
I am God's heritage. (1 Pet. 5:3)
I am complete in Christ. (Col. 2:10)
I am forever free from sin's power. (Rom. 6:14)
I am sanctified. (1 Cor. 6:11)
I am loved eternally. (1 Pet. 1:5)
I am kept in the palm of His hand. (John 10:29)
I am kept from falling. (Jude 1:24)
I am not condemned. (Rom. 8:1-2; 1 Cor. 11:32)
I am one with the Lord. (1 Cor. 6:17)
I am quickened by His mighty power. (Eph. 2:1)
I am seated in heavenly places. (Eph. 1:3)
I am light in the darkness. (Matt. 5:14)
I am a candle in a dark place. (Matt. 5:15)
I am a city set on a hill. (Matt. 5:14)
I am the salt of the earth. (Matt. 5:13)
I am His sheep. (John 10:14)
I am a citizen of Heaven. (Phil. 3:20; 1 Pet. 2:11)

I am hidden with Christ in God. (Ps. 32:7)
I am protected from the evil one. (2 Thes. 3:3; 1 John 5:18)
I am kept by the power of God. (1 Pet. 1:5)
I am secure in Christ. (John 10:28-29)
I am set on a Rock. (Ps. 40:2)
I am more than a conqueror. (Rom. 8:37)
I am born again. (1 Pet. 1:23)
I am healed by His stripes. (Isa. 53:6)
I am hidden in the secret place of the Almighty. (Ps. 91:1)
I am a believer, and the light of the Gospel shines in my mind. (2 Cor. 4:4)
I am a branch on Christ's vine. (John 15:5)
I am redeemed from the curse of the law. (Gal. 3:13)
I am a new creation in Christ. (2 Cor. 5:17)
I am who God says I am. (Rom. 3:4)
I am forgiven. (Mt. 26:28)
I am loved. (John. 3:16)
I am the head only, not the tail. (Dt. 28:13)
I am above only, not beneath. (Dt. 28:13)
I am blessed coming and I am blessed going. (Dt. 28:6)
I am filled with the Spirit. (Eph. 5:18)
I am blessed with every spiritual blessing. (Eph. 1:3)
I am the light of the world. (Mt. 5:14)
I am filled with the Spirit. (Acts 2:38)

WHO AM I?
PREPARED
SAINTS
Teachers
Predestined
BRIDE OF CHRIST
CREATED IN THE IMAGE OF GOD
Rooted
Prisoner FOR The LORD
Daughter
Humble
SMART
Wise
FOUND
A CRUCIAL PART OF THE BODY OF CHRIST
Remembered
Blameless
BLESSED
USEFUL
CHILDREN OF GOD
FILLED
Powerful
Baptized
Heirs
Hopeful
MARKED
apostles & prophets
BEAUTIFUL
Brilliant
NOT Guilty
God's Friend
Righteous
SERVANT
WORKMANSHIP
God's People
included
LOVED
ALIENS TO THE WORLD
Brought NEAR
Forgiven
Redeemed
WORKERS 4 CHRIST
SPIRIT
CALLED
NO LONGER captives
Peaceful
Possession
Patient
unified
CHURCH
PASTOR
Evangelist
Built up
Mature
COMPASSIONATE
Raised up w/ Christ
TAUGHT
We ARE THE Children of the LIGHT
Gifted
Steady
PAINLESS
THANKFUL
Rich
ALIVE
KIND
SEALED
IMITATOR OF God
Princess
JOYFUL
Recievers OF CHRIST'S LOVE
FILLED WITH THE KNOWLELEDGE OF CHRIST
ATTAINING

Doodle Page

Doodle Page

WHEN JESUS DECLARED "I AM"

John 6:35, Then Jesus declared, "I am the bread of life. He who comes to me will never go hungry, and he who believes in me will never be thirsty.

John 8:12, When Jesus spoke again to the people, he said, "I am the light of the world. Whoever follows me will never walk in darkness, but will have the light of life."

John 10:9, I am the gate; whoever enters through me will be saved. He will come in and go out, and find pasture.

John 10:11, "I am the good shepherd. The good shepherd lays down his life for the sheep."

John 11:25-26, Jesus said to her, "I am the resurrection and the life. He who believes in me will live, even though he dies; and whoever lives and believes in me will never die."

John 14:6, Jesus answered, "I am the way and the truth and the life. No one comes to the Father except through me."

John 15:5, "I am the vine; you are the branches. If a man remains in me and I in him, he will bear much fruit; apart from me you can do nothing."

> Write a prayer to God – tell him how you desire to truly know who you are in Him. Thank Him for being all these to you.

Doodle Page

YOUR ORIGINAL DESIGN - IDNJC

Why is it important to know who you are as God sees you?

Because God says that the righteous are BOLD. But if you always feel like a failure and a loser, you will never be BOLD for God because you will never feel good enough to be His hands and feet.

But that is a lie! The devil would love to keep you in that prison of feeling condemned and tearing yourself down all the time! Because you cannot do what God has for you if you don't step into your TRUE IDENTITY! Your IDNJC! Stop trying to become who you already are!

> *"I have nothing to prove, because I am already approved."*
> — STEVEN FURTICK

Your identity is in Jesus Christ! Period. No labels. No sin. No nothing can steal from you who you are in Him! BOOM!

PROVERBS 28:1

The wicked flee when no one pursues, but the righteous are bold as a lion.

2 CORINTHIANS 5:21

For our sake he made him to be sin who knew no sin, so that in him we might become the righteousness of God.

Check out this LeCrae song,

"IDENTITY"
(feat. Da' T.R.U.T.H. & J.R.)

"Hair, check!
Shoes, check!
A brand new fit, lookin' cool, check!
I'm lookin' in the mirror like oooh, yes!
To cover for an insecure dude, check!
But she won't feel me and they won't like me
If I ain't in them J's or them brand new nikes
Let's dig deeper inside my psyche
When it's all said and done even I don't like me

He live in the gym and his hair stay faded
Late model car so they think he made it
He's Christian, he gave his life
But he still ain't satisfied in the savior Christ
Still finds his identity in looks and cars
If he only knew that he ain't have to look so hard
If he looked in God
It may seem odd
But he be so satisfied, he can leave it all

I'm not the shoes I wear
I'm not the clothes I buy
I'm not the house I live in
I'm not the car I drive, no

I'm not the job I work
You can't define my worth
By nothing on God's green earth
My identity is found in Christ, is found in Christ

Got her hair done, toes, nails
Is that Her, well it's hard to tell
Cause she's so caked up in all that make up
It's like she tryna make up for what she ain't but,
She's a saint, but so confused
Cause she's been rejected by all these dudes
That tell her on a scale of 10 she's a two
But that ain't true
If she only knew
In Christ she is loved, she secure and accepted
Never be rejected by God whose elected her
Her beauty is her Godliness
And she ain't gotta flaunt it cause it's obvious
Identity is found in the God we trust
And any other identity will self-destruct
Identity is found in the God we trust
And any other identity will self-destruct

Hey, how do I gain success
Why do I say I'm blessed, huh
Is it the car that I drive
Or the place that I rest
Or the way that I dress, now, now
Is the cause of my pride

*The stage and the set
Or my face in the press, now, now
It's the applause that dies
When the praise is less
If my face is depressed, then, then
It's cause my value and worth is in the volume of the work I produce in the booth
It's a prize and a curse if defined by the perks when the truth is through
Man I won't feel like I don't want to live no more, no more, no more
Cause they don't like me, like they did in 04, 04, 04
So I swallow my pride empowered by God,
I'm complete in Him
He's got peace God's priest, I'm in
In His presence weak is strength
Meet His kin
We His brethren
Read this list
Me forgiven
He's dismissed guilt and my sin
And then I find my worth cause I'm Jesus' friend*

*I'm not the shoes I wear
I'm not the clothes I buy
I'm not the house I live in
I'm not the car I drive, no*

*I'm not the job I work
You can't define my worth
By nothing on God's green earth
My identity is found in Christ, is found in Christ!"*

> "My Righteousness is just as good as Jesus' Righteousness, because it IS Jesus' Righteousness!"
> — E. W. KENYON

> WHEW! If only this song was planted deep within your heart and mind, imagine your new confident self! Would you be bolder, stronger, or value yourself more than ever? Who would you stand up to that you have backed down to in the past? Who would you include that you currently exclude? Who would you forgive that you are currently bitter towards?
>
> Write it down here:

Doodle Page

DO YOU KNOW HOW YOU MOVE GOD?

Look at how much God loves and delights in YOU!

PSALM 149:4

For the LORD takes pleasure in his people; he adorns the humble with salvation.

ZEPHANIAH 3:17 AMP

The Lord your God is in the midst of you, a Mighty One, a Savior [Who saves]! He will rejoice over you with joy; He will rest [in silent satisfaction] and in His love He will be silent and make no mention [of past sins, or even recall them]; He will exult over you with singing.

These are the lyrics to Do You Know the Way You Move Me by Misty Edwards. I believe it is a prophetic song of God singing over you. Read and let the words sink deep as His love encounters YOU today!

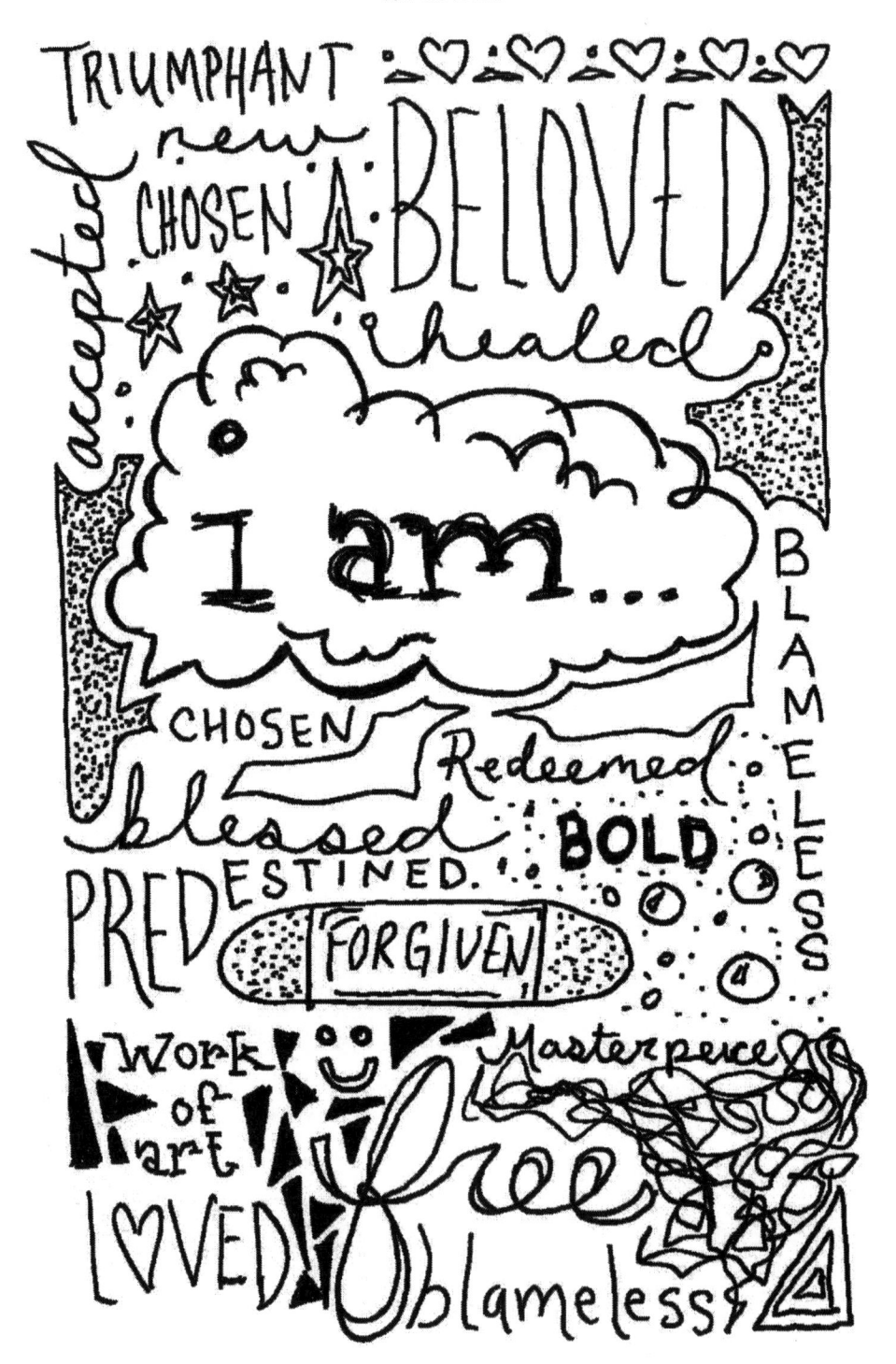

I am...

TRIUMPHANT, new, CHOSEN, BELOVED, accepted, healed, BLAMELESS, CHOSEN, Redeemed, blessed, BOLD, PREDESTINED, FORGIVEN, work of art, Masterpiece, free, LOVED, blameless

DO YOU KNOW THE WAY YOU MOVE ME
by Misty Edwards

And I hear heaven reply
As He's singing over you
I hear heaven reply. He said...
Do you know
how you've caught my eye?
In the secret place
Where you chose to die
He says... Do you know
How you've caught my eye?
In the secret place
Where you chose to be mine

(He says) I saw you there, longing to be mine
Even in the night time,
I saw you reaching out to me
And you said God,
"my flesh is weak but my spirit is willing"
Help me Love.

And I heard your prayer,
I saw you and all your friends; even your family say
"why don't you just walk away?"
Sometimes everything inside of you says
"To go the other way"
But don't give up, No! No!, Don't give in.
In the dark night of faith
You kept on pressing in.

Oh beloved, Do you know
How you've caught my eye?
In the secret place
Where you chose to die

Do you know
How you've caught my eye?
In the secret place
Where you chose to be mine.

Cos, I remember the vows of your youth
And I remember you, when you were just a child
And you look up to sky and you said
If you really there God, I wanna love you.
And saw creation and something in your heart said
I wanna be His.

And even in the middle of nowhere
where you had to stand alone ...Still.
You said I belong to Him and He belong to me.

And I saw you turned away some of those relationships
And even when your heart broke, you said...
I want you more Lord, I want you more than that.

And I saw you denying your flesh
When everything inside of you is screaming.
You said No. I want to show love
And you fought the fight.
Even when you cannot see, still you believe.

And I say, I say Angels, Oh Angels, Oh Angels
Look and see! Look and See
In that dark night of faith they're still loving me.
He says Angels, Oh Angels
Look and see. She said Yes; He said Yes

And He spins around wildly rejoicing
Like a bridegroom will rejoices over a bride
She said Yes; He said Yes
And He rejoices about us like a bridegroom
Can you hear the voice of the Bridegroom
As He sings over you; as He sings over you
Rejoicing. Oh

Do you know the way you've move me.
You've ravished my heart with one glance of your eye
You move my heart; Turn all away for me
Your rising overwhelms me,
Your beautiful tears as lovely as Jerusalem
Oh, as soon as your Love's banner rises, overwhelm me.

> *Do you know the way YOU move God? Write down some of the wonderful ways you have blessed the Lord. Maybe you have failed hard, but yet you continue to praise Him – write this down! Stop looking at your failures and start looking at your God.*

Doodle Page

THE ORIGINAL DESIGN OF OTHERS

It wasn't until after I was married to Ty that I realized that His identity was found in Christ also. I mean, at this point, I really believed I was a masterpiece, but it almost made me fall out of my chair the day I realized God thought this man was a Masterpiece too! WHAT?! Are you kidding me?

Think of someone that annoys you. Think of someone who has hurt you. Think of a famous person.

All of these people, no matter how you feel about them, are truly loved by God. God sent Jesus to die for the meanest person you know! He loves them. Get this: Your parents are a Masterpiece! IKR!!??

> "The body of Christ has bones, not bricks."
> — CRAIG GROESCHEL

Imagine what a swag world we would live in if we all saw each other as Christ sees us!!!!

> *Is there someone you dislike right now that you should ask God for healing and love and respect for? Use the space below to write down what you are thankful for about those people. Consider writing down their identity in Christ and mailing them a letter to share what God thinks of them. Refer back to the IDNJC Chart for this if you need more than the ones listed below.*

MAKE THIS YOUR CONFESSION OVER THEM. (WRITTEN BY KATHLEEN HILDENBRAND)

_____ is who God says He/she is.

_____ is the head only and not the tail.

_____ is above only and not beneath.

_____ is blessed coming and _____ is blessed going.

_____ is chosen by God.

_____ is blessed with every spiritual blessing.

_____ is free forever from sin's power.

_____ is not condemned.

_____ is His sheep.

_____ is a citizen of Heaven.

_____ is a city on a hill.

_____ is the light of the world.

_____ is a new creation in Christ.

_____ is a child of God.

_____ is more-than-a-conqueror.

THE ORIGINAL DESIGN OF OTHERS

_____ is protected from the evil one.

_____ hears His voice.

_____ can do all things through Christ Jesus.

_____ can declare liberty to the captives.

_____ can overcome the enemy.

_____ cannot be moved.

_____ cannot be condemned.

_____ cannot be separated from the love of God.

_____ cannot be taken out of the Father's hand.

_____ has a hope that is sure.

_____ has access to the Father.

_____ has peace with God.

_____ has authority over the enemy.

> *We plan to pray over YOUR parents! We have the opportunity to encounter them with new eyes…with God's eyes!*

iKanministries.com

people build up walls
not to keep others out,
but to see who cares enough
to
break them down

Doodle Page

Doodle Page

IDOL WORSHIP

Everyone worships something because we were originally created to worship God! Some people worship other people, maybe a super star, food, money, things, hobbies, friends, boy/girl-friends, children, parents, Pastors, etc.

Anything you set above your God is an idol. If we don't worship Him, the rocks will cry out!

LUKE 19:40 AMP

He replied, I tell you that if these keep silent, the very stones will cry out.

Jimmy Needham wrote the song Clear the Stage. Check it out.

"CLEAR THE STAGE"

Clear the stage and set the sound and lights ablaze
If that's the measure you must take to crush the idols
Jerk the pews and all the decorations, too
Until the congregation's few, then have revival
Tell your friends that this is where the party ends
Until you're broken for your sins, you can't be social
Then seek the Lord and wait for what he has in store
And know that great is your reward so just be hopeful

'Cause you can sing all you want to
Yes, you can sing all you want to
You can sing all you want to

And still get it wrong; worship is more than a song
Take a break from all the plans that you have made
And sit at home alone and wait for god to whisper
Beg him please to open up his mouth and speak
And pray for real upon your knees until they blister
Shine the light on every corner of your life
Until the pride and lust and lies are in the open
Then read the word and put to test the things you've heard
Until your heart and soul are stirred and rocked and broken

'Cause you can sing all you want to
Yes, you can sing all you want to
You can sing all you want to
And still get it wrong; worship is more than a song

We must not worship something that's not even worth it
Clear the stage, make some space for the one who deserves it

Anything I put before my God is an idol
Anything I want with all my heart is an idol
Anything I can't stop thinking of is an idol
Anything that I give all my all my love is an idol

'Cause I can sing all I want to
Yes, I can sing all I want to
And we can sing all we want to
And we can sing all we want to
We can sing all we want to
And still get it wrong
Worship is more than a song

Clear the stage and set the sound and lights ablaze
If that's the measure you must take to crush the idols

> **What Idols do you have in your life? List them here.**

Doodle Page

Doodle Page

IS GOD YOUR FIRST

Read Deuteronomy 6:4-9 and Matthew 22:34-40.

Where are you today? "Where there is no vision [no redemptive revelation of God], the people perish" (Proverbs 29:18a AMP). Be real with your answers — whether good, bad, ugly, or great. Underline where you are today. Circle where you would like to be in one year.

1. Based on the way you live today (i.e., spend your time and money), how well would you say that you are loving God with all your heart, mind, soul, and strength?

    - Never
    - Sometimes
    - Many times
    - Consistently
    - Always

2. On an average day, is your relationship with God cold, lukewarm, or hot? Take a look at Revelation 3:15-16. Where are you?

    - Losing momentum
    - Flat
    - Growing slowly
    - Growing quickly
    - Soaring

MATTHEW 11:28-30

Come to me, all you who are weary and burdened, and I will give you rest. Take my yoke upon you and learn from me, for I am gentle and humble in heart, and you will find rest for your souls. For my yoke is easy and my burden is light.

> *Make this your prayer. Submit to God. Confess to Him if He is not your first love. Tell Him you desperately want to love Him like that.*
>
> *Lay down whatever sin, or burden is stealing from you loving God fully.*

Doodle Page

Doodle Page

WORSHIP IS A RESPONSE

Worship is an overflow from my heart.
It is a response to God's vast love for me.

When you walk into God's sanctuary (the church or wherever), He is there. We don't worship because we feel like it. We worship because He is WORTHY! Worthy is the lamb who took my place. Right?!!!

If we don't worship Him the rocks will cry out!

We are warriors changing the atmosphere every place we move! We are secure in the one who bought us freedom! So when we walk in, pray in the spirit! Bring the fire of God. Bring a love encounter! Bring all your gifts to the altar of God.

Don't make your sold out worship dependent on how great the music is or isn't. Don't make it based on you! Don't worship because you feel like it.

Worship because you have been redeemed from the pit of hell. Worship because it changes the atmosphere. Worship because it's your calling. Worship because God made you to influence kingdoms and nations! You're a leader worshipper whether you're on a stage, in your seat, in the bathroom, the kitchen, a restaurant, in the closet, doing the dishes, or at an activity! You are!

Be who you already are and stop striving so hard to become something when you're already awesome!! It's already IN you!

MAKE THIS YOUR WORSHIP CONFESSION.

24/7 WORSHIP DECLARATION
BY KATHLEEN RAY HILDENBRAND

I was created to worship
My worship is powerful
My gifts and talents are from God and for God
I am worthy to lead people in worship

My worship is a pleasing aroma to Father God
He delights in me and I delight in Him
I don't worship for man's approval
I worship for an audience of one

WORSHIP IS A RESPONSE

I am a worship warrior
When I come into agreement with God, atmospheres are transformed
Chains are broken and the captives are set free
I am called to build up and encourage the body through worship

Worship is not just the song on my lips
It is the obedience of my heart
I will worship God through every move I make
I will stand firm against the attacks of the enemy

I will remember what God has done
I won't forget the miracles I have seen
I will worship God day and night and night and day
His praise will be continuously on my lips

I will stand in unity with the heart of God
I will call things as they aren't as though they are
I will see the broken walls of my life restored
I will give God all the honor and glory.

WORSHIP

Write a prayer to God about your true desire to worship Him.

Doodle Page

SUPER POWER TO WITNESS

You were created to GO into all the world. However, ask God where your place is. Acts 1:8 says it starts at home. Are you an excellent role model for siblings, friends, etc.? Are you quickly obedient to your parents? Are you praying over family, friends and forgiving quickly where you are? You must start where you are because until you are trustworthy with the LITTLE you have now, you cannot be entrusted with more.

He who is faithful in a very little [thing] is faithful also in much, and he who is dishonest and unjust in a very little [thing] is dishonest and unjust also in much. Luke 16:10

Look at this power that you have been given to minister at home first and then into all the world!

ACTS 1:8 AMPLIFIED BIBLE (AMP)

But you shall receive power (ability, efficiency, and might) when the Holy Spirit has come upon you, and you shall be My witnesses in Jerusalem and all Judea and Samaria and to the ends (the very bounds) of the earth.

Have you ever thrown a rock into water? What do you see? Yes, ripples. Ripples start at the point of impact and continue out from that point. Ripples don't expand in reverse. You can't skip a ripple.

Jesus faithfully empowered and called us, His disciples, to be witnesses. Jesus began the Great Ripple that would eventually reach you and me some two-thousand years later!

A similar effect can be true for us. What if an outreach effort began with you?

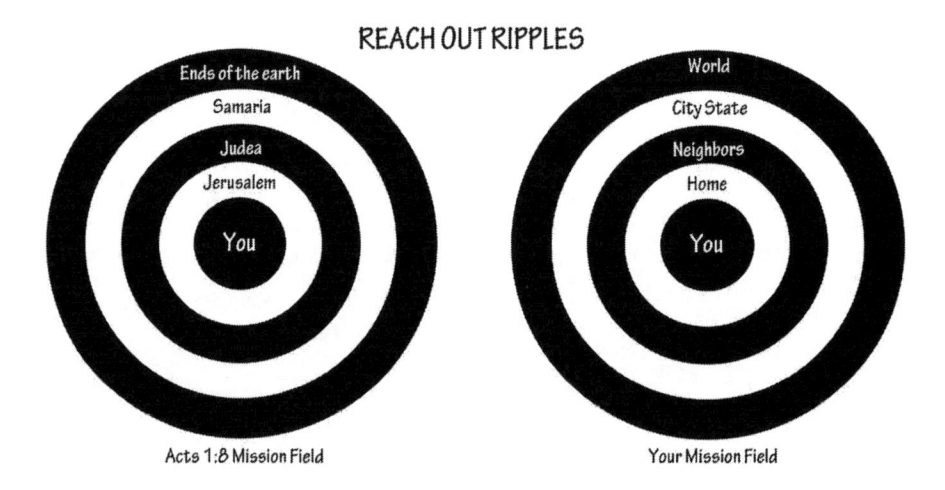

REACH OUT RIPPLES

Acts 1:8 Mission Field (Ends of the earth, Samaria, Judea, Jerusalem, You)

Your Mission Field (World, City State, Neighbors, Home, You)

When you throw a rock into water, you cannot stop it from making ripples. It's a natural process. This should happen to you as well. As the power and love of God transforms you, you will accidently love people more than you ever could on purpose.

Once your heart is in love with God, reaching out is a supernatural response, not a dutiful work. It becomes who you are.

> Imagine the mighty ripples that can take place when God's uses you to LOVE others—to reach out into your neighborhood, your city, our state.
>
> Often, reaching out starts with those closest to you and eventually works its way outward. But it takes time and God's power to multiply!

Start at home. Too many people minister to others while their home life is on the verge of breaking apart.

You cannot effectively minister until you lose your life. It is in losing your life that you find it (Read Matthew 16:25).

Jesus proclaimed in John 12:24, "I tell you the truth, unless a kernel of wheat falls to the ground and dies, it remains only a single seed. But if it dies, it produces many seeds."

EVALUATE YOUR MISSION FIELDS:

My Heart

Has God invaded my life and radically changed me? Do I seek God daily in prayer and in His Word? If you are reading this, then most likely, you are seeking God. When this study ends, will your pursuit continue?

Home

How's my home life? Am I respectful and honoring of others in my home (my spouse, children, siblings, or parents)? Do I serve lovingly, without selfish motives? If you said "no" to any of these questions, it's time to start being a minister in your home.

Neighbors

Do your neighbors love and follow Christ? If not, write their names down on a list and pray for them. Ask God to reveal ways to minister to them. Maybe you need to start by meeting your neighbors!

To me, neighbors are also the people with whom we share our daily life—co-workers, a housekeeper, the dry-cleaners, the grocer, extended family, friends, school buddies, teammates, the local treatment center, and so on. Are you serving and sharing the love of Christ with your neighbors? Write down a few ways to demonstrate love to them.

City or State

Do you know the needs and opportunities in your city? If you haven't already researched this, maybe it's time to get started.

What is the teen pregnancy rate? Is there a prison ministry in your area? How many foster kids or homeless people are there in your state? Are there ministries that feed and provide for local impoverished families—and do they need volunteers or other assistance?

You will not know how to serve if you don't know the needs and the opportunities in your own state.

World

Some people are called to live in a foreign nation to develop Christ-followers. Is this you?

Whether you're called to live abroad or not, there are many ways to have a global impact right from your home.

TWO WAYS TO HELP YOU START TODAY:

- *Pray!* There are many resources that can help direct you in what and how to pray. One of my favorites is the VOM (Voice of the Martyrs) Prayer Calendar, which is now available as a phone application for iPhone and Android.
- *Give!* You can give money to help dig water wells, provide disaster relief, fight human trafficking, sponsor a child, or support a missionary. You don't have to be wealthy to make a difference. Your generosity will make Kingdom ripples no matter the amount!

> *Write down 3 ways you can minister in your own family/home life and sustain it.*

Doodle Page

DO YOU WANT A SUPER POWER

After Jesus ascended, He sent HIS Spirit, called the Holy Spirit, to live IN you! The timing over receiving the spirit is a very controversial issue. It seems like denominations have been formed so that they can battle over what they believe about the timing. But in John 17, Jesus last words, He ask us to be unified, so it is completely ridiculous to argue over the subject.

However, what is important is that you have this superpower.

You may have it and not know it. You may be saved and not have it.

You can receive the Holy Spirit when you are saved, but some receive it later. I am not sure why, but I can tell you this. If you do not operate in power and faithfulness, maybe you haven't received it yet. If you are not sure, let us ask for it because we know if we ask, He will give it. He's a good Father.

ACTS 19:2

And he asked them, Did you receive the Holy Spirit when you believed [on Jesus as the Christ]? And they said, No, we have not even heard that there is a Holy Spirit.

There's a reason why Paul asked this person if they received the Spirit when they first believed. The reason why is because some of us do receive the Spirit when we first believe the Bible says that, but sometimes we don't.

ACTS 2:38 AMP

And Peter answered them, Repent (change your views and purpose to accept the will of God in your inner selves instead of rejecting it) and be baptized, every one of you, in the name of Jesus Christ for the forgiveness of and release from your sins; and you shall receive the gift of the Holy Spirit.

For me personally, Acts 2:38 describes exactly how I received the Spirit. I was a believer in Jesus Christ. I was completely committed to following his ways and becoming a better person. I no longer wanted to walk in sin and I didn't hang out with my old friends anymore. I changed my places and my faces that I spent time with because I wanted to be transformed into the image of Christ. And I knew that my old ways and my old company would correct my ability to do so.

I served, I read my Bible, I worked very hard to become more like Christ, but it didn't seem to get me anywhere. I was a worrier and I lacked peace. I was not calm, I gossiped, I was hypercritical of nearly everyone I knew.

I believe I was foolishly critical and judgmental, tearing down people because I had not yet forgiven myself for my past repulsive behavior. I never felt completely free from my past darkness.

In fact, I remember begging God over and over again to please forgive me. What I didn't know until late one night when I was at a Bible study seeking after the heart of God, was that God had already forgiven me. The problem was that I have not forgiven myself.

Have you ever felt two-faced, horrible – like a mixed up good friend and bad person all in one? That was me! Ask God to forgive you, then receive it!

Receiving the Spirit When You First Believed

ACTS 19:2 AMPLIFIED BIBLE (AMP)

And he asked them, Did you receive the Holy Spirit when you believed [on Jesus as the Christ]? And they said, No, we have not even heard that there is a Holy Spirit.

1 CORINTHIANS 12:13 AMPLIFIED BIBLE (AMP)

For by [means of the personal agency of] one [Holy] Spirit we were all, whether Jews or Greeks, slaves or free, baptized [and by baptism united together] into one body, and all made to drink of one [Holy] Spirit.

RECEIVING THE SPIRIT WHEN BORN AGAIN

EZEKIEL 36:26 AMPLIFIED BIBLE (AMP)

A new heart will I give you and a new spirit will I put within you, and I will take away the stony heart out of your flesh and give you a heart of flesh.

> *Did you receive the Spirit when you first believed? If not, ask. Pray. He is a good Father.*

Doodle Page

Doodle Page

SECRET LANGUAGE

Did you know that God has a secret language that you and He can speak together…Only He knows what you are saying. Almost no one around you can understand. Your enemy cannot understand.

Have you ever felt weak inside? Maybe something is too hard to finish or you feel very, very sad about something? Well, God gave you a GIFT – a way to strengthen you from the INSIDE out!

This secret language makes your inner man strong! It is not for showing off or letting everyone know what you have. It's not for public display. Everyone desires to be strong that is why I believe there are so many super hero movies! This language strengthens you like you strengthen your muscles at the gym!

STRENGTHENING THE INNER MAN

2 CORINTHIANS 4:16 AMPLIFIED BIBLE (AMP)

Therefore we do not become discouraged (utterly spiritless, exhausted, and wearied out through fear). Though our outer man is [progressively] decaying and wasting away, yet our inner self is being [progressively] renewed day after day.

ROMANS 7:22 AMPLIFIED BIBLE (AMP)

For I endorse and delight in the Law of God in my inmost self [with my new nature].

EPHESIANS 3:16 AMPLIFIED BIBLE (AMP)

May He grant you out of the rich treasury of His glory to be strengthened and reinforced with mighty power in the inner man by the [Holy] Spirit [Himself indwelling your innermost being and personality].

EPHESIANS 6:18 AMPLIFIED BIBLE (AMP)

Pray at all times (on every occasion, in every season) in the Spirit, with all [manner of] prayer and entreaty. To that end keep alert and watch with strong purpose and perseverance, interceding in behalf of all the saints (God's consecrated people).

ROMANS 8:26-27 AMPLIFIED BIBLE (AMP)

So too the [Holy] Spirit comes to our aid and bears us up in our weakness; for we do not know what prayer to offer nor how to offer it worthily as we ought, but the Spirit Himself goes to meet our supplication and pleads in our behalf with unspeakable yearnings and groanings too deep for utterance. 27 And He Who searches the hearts of men knows what is in the mind of the [Holy] Spirit [what His intent is], because the Spirit intercedes and pleads [before God] in behalf of the saints according to and in harmony with God's will.

JUDE 20 AMPLIFIED BIBLE (AMP)

But you, beloved, build yourselves up [founded] on your most holy faith [make progress, rise like an edifice higher and higher], praying in the Holy Spirit;

1 CORINTHIANS 14:2, 13-15, 39 AMPLIFIED BIBLE (AMP)

For one who speaks in an [unknown] tongue speaks not to men but to God, for no one understands or catches his meaning, because in the [Holy] Spirit he utters secret truths and hidden things [not obvious to the understanding]. 13 Therefore, the person who speaks in an [unknown] tongue should pray [for the power] to interpret and explain what he says. 14 For if I pray in an [unknown] tongue, my spirit [by the Holy Spirit within me] prays, but my mind is unproductive [it bears no fruit and helps nobody]. 15 Then what am I to do? I will pray with my spirit [by the Holy Spirit that is within me], but I will also pray [intelligently] with my mind and understanding; I will sing with my spirit [by the Holy Spirit that is within me], but I will sing [intelligently] with my mind and understanding also. 39 So [to conclude], my brethren, earnestly desire and set your hearts on prophesying (on being inspired to preach and teach and to interpret God's will and purpose), and do not forbid or hinder speaking in [unknown] tongues.

PRAYING IN TONGUES

MARK 16:17 AMPLIFIED BIBLE (AMP)

17 And these attesting signs will accompany those who believe: in My name they will drive out demons; they will speak in new languages;

1 CORINTHIANS 12:4-11 AMPLIFIED BIBLE (AMP)

Now there are distinctive varieties and distributions of endowments (gifts, extraordinary powers distinguishing certain Christians, due to the power of divine grace operating in their souls by the Holy Spirit) and they vary, but the [Holy] Spirit remains the same. 5 And there are distinctive varieties of service and ministration, but it is the same Lord [Who is served]. 6 And there are distinctive varieties of operation [of working to accomplish things], but it is the same God Who inspires and energizes them all in all. 7 But to each one is given the manifestation of the [Holy] Spirit [the evidence, the spiritual illumination of the Spirit] for good and profit. 8 To one is given in and through the [Holy] Spirit [the power to speak] a message of wisdom, and to another [the power to express] a word of knowledge and understanding according to the same [Holy] Spirit; 9 To another [wonder-working] faith by the same [Holy] Spirit, to another the extraordinary powers of healing by the one Spirit; 10 To another the working of miracles, to another prophetic insight (the gift of interpreting the divine will and purpose); to another the ability to discern and distinguish between [the utterances of true] spirits [and false ones], to another various kinds of [unknown] tongues, to another the ability to interpret [such] tongues. 11 All these [gifts, achievements, abilities] are inspired and brought to pass by one and the same [Holy] Spirit, Who apportions to each person individually [exactly] as He chooses.

ACTS 2:4 AMPLIFIED BIBLE (AMP)

And they were all filled (diffused throughout their souls) with the Holy Spirit and began to speak in other (different, foreign) languages (tongues), as the Spirit kept giving them clear and loud expression [in each tongue in appropriate words].

EPHESIANS 6:18-19 AMPLIFIED BIBLE (AMP)

Pray at all times (on every occasion, in every season) in the Spirit, with all [manner of] prayer and entreaty. To that end keep alert and watch with strong purpose and perseverance, interceding in behalf of all the saints (God's consecrated people). 19 And [pray] also for me, that [freedom of] utterance may be given me, that I may open my mouth to proclaim boldly the mystery of the good news (the Gospel),

> *Review these verses and discuss with the Lord what it means to pray in the Spirit. Ask Him for wisdom and revelation to know Him better and what this means to you and in your life.*
>
> *Also consider discussing with your leader and your parents.*

Doodle Page

FORGIVE QUICKLY

MARK 11:25-26 AMPLIFIED BIBLE (AMP)

And whenever you stand praying, if you have anything against anyone, forgive him and let it drop (leave it, let it go), in order that your Father Who is in heaven may also forgive you your [own] failings and shortcomings and let them drop. But if you do not forgive, neither will your Father in heaven forgive your failings and shortcomings.

What if someone you knew ended up in hell because you were bitter and unforgiving towards them? Wouldn't that be awful? What if you ended up in hell because someone didn't forgive you? Now, that brings a whole new level of awful, doesn't it?

But many times do we hold grudges, tell people we will never forgive them, or cut people out of our lives (usually by unfriending them or unfollowing them on Instagram? Yes, I know some of you have done that to me).

We have been forgiven so much how arrogant is it to say that someone else's sins are worse than ours! Shame on all of us because we know we have ALL done it!

Some of you don't know this, but I was abused for four years in my home. I didn't feel safe there. I hated it and hated myself because of it. But God! Today, I have fully forgiven the man who hurt me so much! MY unforgiveness didn't hurt him; it hurt me. When I forgave him (although he never asked), I felt FREE!

FORGIVE

> *Who do you need to forgive FULLY? Who do you need to ask for forgiveness from? Who do you need to re-follow on Instagram? ☺ Do it. Just do it. Stop holding off. Repent to God. Ask Him to heal your heart.*

Doodle Page

Doodle Page

WORK WITH OTHERS —NOT ALONE

If Jesus needed others in His life, how much more do we? You can do some good on your own, but being part of a team will bring a far greater impact! Increase the Kingdom's influence by working alongside others for a common goal. Multiply!

ECCLESIASTES 4:9-12

Two are better than one, because they have a good return for their work: If one falls down, his friend can help him up. But pity the man who falls and has no one to help him up! Also, if two lie down together, they will keep warm. But how can one keep warm alone? Though one may be overpowered, two can defend themselves. A cord of three strands is not quickly broken.

ANSWER THESE QUESTIONS:

- Who are you doing life with?

- Are you serving alongside other believers as a team?

- Who's on your life's board of directors? These people are significant and direct voices in your life. Have you told them that they sit on your board?

- Are you in a consistent small-group with other believers?

- Do you have a friend who holds you accountable?

- Is there someone committed to pray for and with you?

- Do you have a mentor/mentee relationship with someone?

- Are you intentionally engaged and encouraging with those living in your home?

- Are you a good friend to have?

- Do you include or exclude others?

- Are you sepnding time with people who help you grow in the Lord or pull you into corrupted behavior?

- Are you an encourager or do you tear down others with jokes and sarcasm?

If you need more community, ask God to lead you to the right relationships. He will show you if there's a person or group with whom you need to connect.

Life is BETTER together

WORK WITH OTHERS not alone.

Doodle Page

GREAT COMMISSION PRACTICE ROUND

Before Jesus left the disciples to do their work without Him, He trained them under His wing. They walked with Him and then he propelled them on a practice round. We know that this practice was powerful because when He left them to themselves (of course, with His Holy Spirit) they were able to reach our generation all these years later!

We will be practicing together also like Jesus did with His disciples. Notice that He didn't send them alone so we won't work alone either. We will pray over our parents – well at least the parents of your friends. We will also have the opportunity to listen to God about your parents Original Design. But then, guess what? We are stepping out of our comfortable place – no more practice. We will do this for complete strangers. Listening to Jesus instructions was crucial for the Disciples. Listening to God will be crucial for us as well!

> *Read through these instructions and jot down the details so that you can practice listening to instructions.*

LUKE 10:1-23

After this the Lord appointed seventy-two others and sent them on ahead of him, two by two, into every town and place where he himself was about to go. 2 And he said to them, "The harvest is plentiful, but the laborers are few. Therefore pray earnestly to the Lord of the harvest to send out laborers into his harvest. 3 Go your way; behold, I am sending you out as lambs in the midst of wolves. 4 Carry no moneybag, no knapsack, no sandals, and greet no one on the road. 5 Whatever house you enter, first say, 'Peace be to this house!' 6 And if a son of peace is there, your peace will rest upon him. But if not, it will return to you. 7 And remain in the same house, eating and drinking what they provide, for the laborer deserves his wages. Do not go from house to house. 8 Whenever you enter a town and they receive you, eat what is set before you. 9 Heal the sick in it and say to them, 'The kingdom of God has come near to you.' 10 But whenever you enter a town and they do not receive you, go into its streets and say, 11 'Even the dust of your town that clings to our feet we wipe off against you. Nevertheless know this, that the kingdom of God has come near.' 12 I tell you, it will be more bearable on that day for Sodom than for that town. 13 "Woe to you, Chorazin! Woe to you, Bethsaida! For if the mighty works done in you had been done in Tyre and Sidon, they would have repented long ago, sitting in sackcloth and ashes. 14 But it will be more bearable in the judgment for Tyre and Sidon than for you. 15 And you, Capernaum, will you be exalted to heaven? You shall be brought down to Hades. 16 "The one who hears you hears me, and the one who rejects you rejects me, and the one who rejects me rejects him who sent me." 17 The seventy-two returned with joy, saying, "Lord, even the demons are subject to us in your name!" 18 And he said to them, "I saw Satan fall like lightning from heaven. 19 Behold, I have given you authority to tread on serpents and scorpions, and over all the power of the enemy, and nothing shall hurt you. 20 Nevertheless, do not rejoice in this, that the spirits are subject to you, but rejoice that your names are written in heaven." 21 In that same hour he rejoiced in the

Holy Spirit and said, "I thank you, Father, Lord of heaven and earth, that you have hidden these things from the wise and understanding and revealed them to little children; yes, Father, for such was your gracious will. 22 All things have been handed over to me by my Father, and no one knows who the Son is except the Father, or who the Father is except the Son and anyone to whom the Son chooses to reveal him." 23 Then turning to the disciples he said privately, "Blessed are the eyes that see what you see!

How well do you listen to your parents instructions? Do you do what they tell you the FIRST time or do you drag your feet? The way you obey your parents can easily reveal a deeper heart issue.

Leaders: You may consider a Hometown missionary trip this section.

"GREAT MOVES OF GOD ARE USUALLY PRECEDED BY SIMPLE ACTS OF OBEDIENCE."

— Steven Furtick

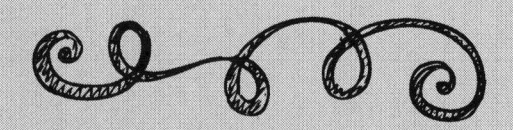

Doodle Page

Doodle Page

DELEGATED AUTHORITY

You – Yes, YOU, have been given authority by God! It is similar to a Police Man who has been given authority by the government to issue tickets and arrest law-breakers, you have been given the authority to use the name of JESUS!

LUKE 10:19 AMP

Behold! I have given you authority and power to trample upon serpents and scorpions, and [physical and mental strength and ability] over all the power that the enemy [possesses]; and nothing shall in any way harm you.

What happens at the NAME of Jesus?

PHILIPPIANS 2:10-11 AMP

That in (at) the name of Jesus every knee should (must) bow, in heaven and on earth and under the earth, 11 And every tongue [frankly and openly] confess and acknowledge that Jesus Christ is Lord, to the glory of God the Father.

RESIST

> *You must use this authority for it to work in you and He is able to do MORE than you can imagine ACCORDING TO _____ What? Read the following and write down in your own words how you can use Jesus name.*

EPHESIANS 3:20 ESV

Now to him who is able to do far more abundantly than all that we ask or think, according to the power at work within us.

Let this song be our confession:

STILL BELIEVE

by Kim Walker-Smith

Your blood makes the deaf to hear right now
Your blood takes away the curse right now
Your blood heals every disease right now
Your blood sets the addict free right now

And I still believe You're the same yesterday, today and forever
And I still believe Your blood is sufficient for me

Your blood mends the broken heart right now
Your blood compels me to forgive right now
Your blood transforms my mind right now
Your blood brings the dead to life right now

You're the higher power
Darkness cannot stand
No longer bound to sin, I am free

All that I need
You are all that I need, Jesus
Your blood is enough for me
I believe.

Cover us right now Jesus
The blood, it opens deaf ears
The blood, breaks down disease
In Your presence, God, it has no place,
Pain has no place, disease has no place, sickness has no place
Weariness has no place, depression has no place
In Your presence, Jesus

We find all we need, In Your presence, Jesus
The Yates family believes.

Let faith rise,
I believe You are who You say You are
You are the one who sees me,
You're the one who's for me, every hair on my head
You created me, how You love me
You're the one who has abundant life for me
You're the one who has joy for me, Jesus
I believe You are all I need

With all my heart, with all I am, even when I cannot see
I will stand with faith and I will believe

I will never stop believing
I believe, You are more than enough for me, God
I will not fear,
Cause I believe
We believe

Doodle Page

HOMETOWN MISSIONARY

"When you know who you are, you will know what to do."

— CRAIG GROESCHEL

You don't need to leave the country to serve because there are hurting people right where you live.

To be a missionary in your everyday life is simply about asking God what He has for you today and carrying it out as you live life. When you visit a friend's, school, work, the park, or the gas station, actively listen for who God has for you to love. (Of course, if you are a minor, check with your parents about safety.) Some suggestions:

- Read the cashier's nametag and call him or her by it. It's shocking how touching it is to hear your own name. Science says that it ignites or lights up every area of the brain.
- Speak encouraging words.
- Ask if they need prayer.
- Ask them if they know Jesus.
- If you see someone, strike up a conversation with them. If God leads you to, ask them if they want to pray.
- Don't fear the rejection of man. It's not you they are rejecting.

> ## "Every setback is a setup for a comeback."
>
> — T. D. JAKES

Another way to live Your Life as a Mission Trip is to pray in advance and ask God who you are looking for. This is an easy start, but then it will become a lifestyle.

1. Pray and complete the chart below.
2. Form groups of three or four.
   - Combine group lists on the right.
   - Each member hold your own list
3. Choose your location – the grocery store, park, skating?
4. Start looking for people to pray for.
5. When someone matches your list, approach slowly with respect and honor…
   - Say something like: "This may seem a little odd, but we prayed and ask God who we should pray for and we think you're on our list."
   - Show them your list. (They may see themselves on your list.)
   - Build rapport. (Ask questions to get to know them.)
   - Let them know God has highlighted them, and wants to bless them.
   - Ask if you can pray for them. '
6. If they say "No"…
   - If they say "No"—Bless them and move to the next opportunity.
7. If they say "Yes'"
   - Pray. Ask if you can set your hand on them. Only touch above the shoulders.

8. Ask them if they would like to have a relationship with Jesus personally.
   - Help them ask Jesus into their life.
   - Jesus, I know that I have sinned against you. Thank you for forgiving me of my sins. I believe that you are the Son of God and the only way to the Father. I receive you as my personal Lord and Savior. Holy Spirit fill me now and continue this good work that you have started in me.
   - If someone is not on your list, but is clearly in need of prayer, don't pass up the opportunity.

BEFORE YOU START COMPLETE THIS:

Pray and Write down anything you hear in the space below.

Location (stop sign, bench digital clock, coffee shop, Target, Wal-Mart, etc.)

_____   _____   _____   _____

_____   _____   _____   _____

Person's name or appearance

_____   _____   _____   _____

_____   _____   _____   _____

What might they need prayer for (knee brace, cane, kidneys, tumor, left ankle, marriage, etc.)

_____   _____   _____   _____

_____   _____   _____   _____

The unusual (lollipop, windmill, lime-green door, dolphins, etc.)

_____   _____   _____   _____

_____   _____   _____   _____

> *Write down some places you can be a hometown missionary.*
>
> *Are you worried you don't hear from God? I was too. It's okay. If you are His, you do hear His voice. Practice being still and listening for it 5 to 15 minutes a day.*

"THE VOICE YOU BELIEVE WILL DETERMINE THE FUTURE YOU EXPERIENCE."

— Steve Furtick

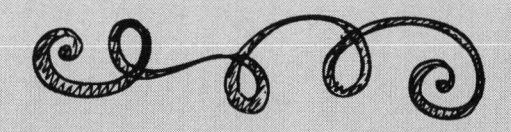

Doodle Page

SPEAK TO YOUR MOUNTAIN

God never told you to pray to Him about your mountain. Of course, you can tell Him about it and cry to Him over it….He is your Comforter! Yes, cry out to Him. Tell Him your struggles.

Have you ever been around someone who it seems like all they can do is complain, complain, complain, complain? Have you sat there and thought, *Hmm I think I could help you figure this out by changing your current behavior to this behavior.* The definition of insanity is doing the same thing over and over again while expecting different results.

This is similar with your spiritual life. Have you ever beat yourself down until you are blue in the face about your struggles, but still continue to do NOTHING about it? Maybe it's time to speak TO your mountain instead of ABOUT your mountain.

The Lord says he will make you into a threshing sledge, new and sharp, with many teeth. You will thresh the mountains and crush them, and reduce the hills to chaff. (Isaiah 41:15) What a promise! How often I add a rock onto my mountain by complaining about a circumstance when I am CALLED to reduce it to dust beneath my feet.

MARK 11:2-24 AMP

In the morning, when they were passing along, they noticed that the fig tree was withered [completely] away to its roots.

And Peter remembered and said to Him, Master, look! The fig tree which You doomed has withered away!

And Jesus, replying, said to them, Have faith in God [constantly]. Truly I tell you, whoever says to this mountain, Be lifted up and thrown into the sea! and does not doubt at all in his heart but believes that what he says will take place, it will be done for him. For this reason I am telling you, whatever you ask for in prayer, believe (trust and be confident) that it is granted to you, and you will [get it].

ACTS 3 AMP

3 Now Peter and John were going up to the temple at the hour of prayer, the ninth hour (three o'clock in the afternoon), 2 [When] a certain man crippled from his birth was being carried along, who was laid each day at that gate of the temple [which is] called Beautiful, so that he might beg for charitable gifts from those who entered the temple. 3 So when he saw Peter and John about to go into the temple, he asked them to give him a gift. 4 And Peter directed his gaze intently at him, and so did John, and said, Look at us! 5 And [the man] paid attention to them, expecting that he was going to get something from them. 6 But Peter said, Silver and gold (money) I do not have; but what I do have, that I give to you: in [the use of] the name of Jesus Christ of Nazareth, walk! 7 Then he took hold of the man's right hand with a firm grip and raised him up. And at once his feet and ankle bones became strong and steady, 8 And leaping forth he stood and began to walk, and he went into the temple with them, walking and leaping and praising God. 9 And all the people saw him walking about and praising God, 10 And they recognized him as the man who usually sat [begging] for alms at the Beautiful Gate of the temple; and they were filled with wonder and amazement (bewilderment, consternation) over what had occurred to him. 11 Now while he [still] firmly clung to Peter and John, all the people in utmost amazement ran together and crowded around them in the covered porch (walk) called Solomon's. 12 And Peter, seeing it, answered the people, You men of Israel, why are you so surprised and wondering at this? Why do you keep staring at us, as though by our [own individual] power or [active] piety we had made this man [able] to walk? 13 The God of Abraham and of Isaac and of Jacob, the God of our forefathers, has glorified His Servant and Son Jesus [doing Him this honor], Whom you indeed delivered up and denied and rejected and disowned in the presence of Pilate, when he had determined to let Him go. 14 But you denied and rejected and disowned the Pure and Holy, the Just and Blameless One, and demanded [the pardon of] a murderer to be granted to you. 15 But you killed the very Source (the Author) of life, Whom God raised from the dead. To this we are witnesses. 16 And His name, through and by faith in His name, has made this man whom you see and recognize well and strong. [Yes] the faith which is through and by Him [Jesus] has given the man this perfect soundness [of body] before all of you.17 And now, brethren, I know that you acted in ignorance [not aware of what you were doing], as did your rulers also. 18 Thus has God fulfilled what He foretold by the mouth of all the prophets, that His Christ (the Messiah) should undergo ill treatment and be afflicted and suffer. 19 So repent (change your mind and purpose); turn around and return [to God], that your sins may be erased (blotted out, wiped clean), that times of refreshing (of recovering from the effects of heat, of reviving with fresh air) may come from the presence of the Lord; 20 And that He may send [to you] the Christ (the Messiah), Who before was designated and appointed for you—even Jesus, 21 Whom heaven must receive [and retain] until the time for the complete restoration of all that God spoke by the mouth of all His holy prophets for ages past [from the most ancient time in the memory of man]. 22 Thus Moses said to the forefathers, The Lord God will raise up for you a Prophet from among your brethren as [He raised up] me; Him you shall listen to and understand by hearing and heed in all things whatever He tells you. 23 And it shall be that every soul that does not listen to and understand by hearing and heed that

Prophet shall be utterly exterminated from among the people. 24 Indeed, all the prophets from Samuel and those who came afterwards, as many as have spoken, also promised and foretold and proclaimed these days. 25 You are the descendants (sons) of the prophets and the heirs of the covenant which God made and gave to your forefathers, saying to Abraham, And in your Seed (Heir) shall all the families of the earth be blessed and benefited. 26 It was to you first that God sent His Servant and Son Jesus, when He raised Him up [provided and gave Him for us], to bless you in turning every one of you from your wickedness and evil ways.

Speak to your Mountain

> *What mountain is currently before you that you have been talking about but you need to speak to and see your mountain thrown into the sea before you?*

Doodle Page

Doodle Page

RESIST THE DEVIL

God never told you that He would resist the devil for you! He simply commanded:

Submit to Him.

Resist the devil.

RESIST

And He will flee from you!

JAMES 4:7

Submit yourselves, then, to God. Resist the devil, and he will flee from you.

Simple. Right? Wrong. If you don't know God in all His goodness, you could accidentally mistake the devil for God. In fact, I have seen people do this before! They were fully sold out to the enemies plan to destroy their lives because they were not 100% convinced of God's fingerprints in their lives!

We must read the WORD – the Bible so that we will know truth from lies. Otherwise, what we refer to as Truth or Trash™!

The Word if the filter for everything we hear. Is it Truth or trash? The only way we can fully know is to listen to God through the Bible! Don't take someone's word for it – that is much like building a house on a shaky foundation!

> *Let us self-evaluate. Pray and ask God to show you the answers to these.*

Have you fully surrendered your life to Jesus?

Have you fully submitted your days to Him? Or are you still holding onto something?

Are you actively resisting the thief – the devil in your life or are you agreeing with him?

"GOD'S ANOINTING IS NOT BASED ON YOUR PERFORMANCE, BUT IF YOU DON'T OPEN THE WORD, YOU'RE STUPID, BECAUSE THAT'S WHERE THE WORDS OF LIFE ARE."

— Andrew Wommack

Doodle Page

TAKE POSSESSION

Much like a hunter goes after his prey, we must take possession or receive God's promises.

In Joshua 1, God told them to get moving –take the land I have already given to you! They hesitated. Why?! Because it was a battle! It's a battle to be a good receiver! We know we don't deserve it and for some reason, we think it would be so much better if we had to earn everything. WRONG. The only thing we have earned is death! Know that you ALREADY are a good receiver or you wouldn't be a Christian! Now, it is TIME to TAKE BACK everyone and every place for GOD's glory!

JOSHUA 1:6-11

Be strong (confident) and of good courage, for you shall cause this people to inherit the land which I swore to their fathers to give them. 7 Only you be strong and very courageous, that you may do according to all the law which Moses My servant commanded you. Turn not from it to the right hand or to the left, that you may prosper wherever you go. 8 This Book of the Law shall not depart out of your mouth, but you shall meditate on it day and night, that you may observe and do according to all that is written in it. For then you shall make your way prosperous, and then you shall deal wisely and have good [b]success. 9 Have not I commanded you? Be strong, vigorous, and very courageous. Be not afraid, neither be dismayed, for the Lord your God is with you wherever you go. 10 Then Joshua commanded the officers of the people, saying, 11 Pass through the camp and command the people, Prepare your provisions, for within three days you shall pass over this Jordan to go in to take possession of the land which the Lord your God is giving you to possess.

Let us make this our confession as we prepare to take back God's territory.

You are a good Father. You are my God who keeps his word. You do not lie. You are faithful throughout all generations. You have overcome the world. You love me. In you, I have peace, freedom, no condemnation, and blessings. You rescue and defend. You brought me the good news. You bind up my broken-heart. You release from darkness for the prisoners. You are my comfort.

You give me a crown of beauty instead of ashes, the oil of joy instead of mourning, and a garment of praise instead of a spirit of despair. I will be called an oak of righteousness for Your glory.

Because I am yours, I will rebuild the ruins and restore devastated place; I will renew the ruined homes and cities that have been devastated for generations. Instead of my shame I will receive a double portion, and instead of disgrace I will rejoice in your inheritance. And so I will inherit a double portion in my land, and everlasting joy will be mine. You are for me not against me. No weapon formed against me can prosper. You have plans to prosper me, not to harm me. Your kindness leads me to repentance. You are love. You live in me. You are my source. You have filled me with the same power that raised Christ from the dead. You have filled me with your Spirit. The fruits of your Spirit live in me! Love, joy, peace, forbearance, kindness, goodness, faithfulness, gentleness and self-control live in me. You have set before me life and death, blessings and curses. Today I choose life, so that my children and I may live. I chose life in my words. I chose to draw on your power. I have been crucified with Christ and I no longer live, but Christ lives in me. The life I now live in the body, I live by faith in the Son of God, who loved me and gave himself for me.

Greater are you within me than he that is in the world. My words have the power of life and death. I do not allow words of death to be spoken out of my mouth.

Father, help me take possession of all your promises because you are worthy.

> *What promise do you need to take possession of TODAY? Don't Delay!*

"FAITH IS JUST THE OPEN DOOR THROUGH WHICH THE LORD COMES. DO NOT SAY, 'I WAS SAVED BY FAITH' OR 'I WAS HEALED BY FAITH.' FAITH DOES NOT SAVE AND HEAL. GOD SAVES AND HEALS THROUGH THAT OPEN DOOR. YOU BELIEVE, AND THE POWER OF CHRIST COMES."

— Smith Wigglesworth

Doodle Page

Doodle Page

ARMED IN ATTITUDE

When the resurrection and the life walks into the room, dead things don't stay dead. That same power is living within you! Do you live every day like it?

To have the attitude of Christ, you must know that you are qualified— not by your training or skill, but by the One Qualifier, the Holy Spirit. You are qualified! Having the attitude of Christ means that you will be interrupted. The attitude of Christ knows this: you are an alien with a new purpose and mission to take back territory for the Kingdom of God. The attitude of

Christ is laying down your will and taking up the will of God—no matter the cost.

> *For he chose us in him before the creation of the world to be holy and blameless in his sight. (Ephesians 1:4)*
>
> *But you will receive power when the Holy Spirit comes on you; and you will be my witnesses (Acts 1:8)*
>
> *Be imitators of God, therefore, as dearly loved children and live a life of love, just as Christ loved us and gave himself up for us as a fragrant offering and sacrifice to God. (Ephesians 5:1-2)*

Attitude of acquisition – to be on a mission to possess or acquire

Christ had the ultimate *Attitude of acquisition!*

> *For God so loved the world that he gave his one and only Son, that whoever believes in him shall not perish but have eternal life. (John 3:16)*
>
> *Father, if you are willing, take this cup from me; yet not my will, but yours be done. (Luke 22:42)*

Confess this aloud:

I will carry an attitude of acquisition.
I know I'm qualified, not by training or skill, but by the Holy Spirit.
I am a connector between God and the lost. I expect to be interrupted. In fact, I schedule time for interruptions.
I am an alien to this world. Everywhere I go, I am on a mission to take back territory for the Kingdom of God.
I lay down my will, my agenda, and my life to take up the will of God no matter the cost to me—in Jesus' name!
I am called to bring people into relationship with the Lord wherever my foot treads.
I am an atmosphere changer. Every where I step, the power of God goes with me in Jesus name.

As a man thinks in his heart, so is he.

PROVERBS 23:7

GREATER THINGS

We are called to do MORE than Jesus did, but this list of Jesus miracles is incomplete. According to John 21:25: "Jesus did many other things as well. If every one of them were written down, I suppose that even the whole world would not have room for the books that would be written."

> *Read these. Study them. Daydream about you doing what Jesus did. What does MORE or greater things look like to you? Ask God to help you live like Jesus did – seeing needs of others and meeting them for God's glory.*

New Testament Recorded Miracles of Jesus with corresponding Scripture passages

1. Born to a virgin (Matthew 1:18-25, Luke 1:26-38)
2. Changing water into wine (John 2:1-11)
3. Healing of the royal official's son (John 4:46-54)
4. Healing of the Capernaum demoniac (Mark 1:21-28, Luke 4:33-37)
5. Healing of Peter's mother-in-law (Matthew 8:14-15, Mark 1:29-31, Luke 4:38-39)
6. Healing the sick during the evening (Matt 8:16, Mark 1:32, Luke 4:40)
7. Catching a large number of fish (Luke 5:3-10)
8. Healing a leper (Matthew 8:1-4; Mark 1:40-45; Luke 5:12-15)
9. Miracle of healing a centurion's servant (Matthew 8:5-13, Luke 7:1-10)
10. Healing a paralyzed man (Matthew 9:1-8, Mark 2:1-12, Luke 5:18-26)
11. Healing a withered hand (Matthew 12:9-14, Mark 3:1-6, Luke 6:6-10)

12. Raising a widow's son (Luke 7:11-17)
13. Calming the storm (Matthew 8:23-27, Mark 4:35-41, Luke 8:22-25)
14. Healing the Gerasene man possessed by demons (Matthew 8:28-32, Mark 5:1-13, Luke 8:26-33)
15. Healing a woman with internal bleeding (Matthew 9:20-22, Mark 5:25-34, Luke 8:43-48)
16. Raising Jairus' daughter (Matthew 9:18-19, 23-25; Mark 5:22-24, 35-43; Luke 8:41-42, 49-56)
17. Healing two blind men (Matthew 9:27-31)
18. Healing a mute demon-possessed man (Matthew 9:32-33)
19. Healing a 38 year invalid (John 5:1-17)
20. Feeding 5,000 men and their families (Mt. 14:16-21, Mark 6:35-44, Luke 9:12-17, John 6:5-14)
21. Walking on water (Matthew 14:22-33, Mark 6:45-52, John 6:16-21)
22. Miraculous healing of many people in Gennesaret (Matthew 14:34-36; Mark 6:53-56)
23. Healing a girl possessed by a demon (Matthew 15:21-28, Mark 7:24-30)
24. Healing a deaf man with a speech impediment (Mark 7:31-37)
25. Feeding the 4,000 men and their families (Matthew 15:29-39, Mark 8:1-10)
26. Healing a blind man (Mark 8:22-26)
27. Healing a man born blind (John 9:1-41)
28. Healing a demon-possessed boy (Matthew 17:14-20, Mark 9:17-29, Luke 9:37-43)
29. Catching a fish with a coin in its mouth (Matthew 17:24-27)
30. Healing a blind and mute man who was demon-possessed (Matthew 12:22-23, Luke 11:14)
31. Healing a woman with an 18-year infirmity (Luke 13:10-13)

32. Healing a man with dropsy (Luke 14:1-6)
33. Healing 10 lepers (Luke 17:11-19)
34. Raising of Lazarus (John 11:1-44)
35. Healing Bartimaeus of blindness (Matthew 20:29-34, Mark 10:46-52, Luke 18:35-43)
36. Jesus curses the fig tree with no fruit (Matthew 21:18-22; Mark 11:12-14, 20-25)
37. Restoring a severed ear (Luke 22:45-54)
38. The resurrection of Jesus (1 Corinthians 15, Matthew 28, Mark 16, Luke 24, John 20)
39. Catching 153 fish (John 21:4-11)
40. The ascension of Jesus (Acts 1:1-11)

Source: http://www.aboutbibleprophecy.com/miracles.htm

> *Look up these miracles. Study them. Get familiar with the way Jesus moved in people's lives.*

Doodle Page

Note Page

Doodle Page

THE GREAT COMMISSION

If you are ever unsure of what God called you to do, I can guarantee you He called you to know Him intimately first and then next to stretch out your life for others to know Him as well. This is referred to as The Great Commission. Jesus commissioned all of us before He left us with the Holy Spirit.

But seek first his kingdom and his righteousness, and all these things will be given to you as well. Matthew 6:33

MATTHEW 28:16-20 AMPLIFIED BIBLE (AMP)

16 Now the eleven disciples went to Galilee, to the mountain to which Jesus had directed and made appointment with them. 17 And when they saw Him, they fell down and worshiped Him; but some doubted. 18 Jesus approached and, breaking the silence, said to them, All authority (all power of rule) in heaven and on earth has been given to Me. 19 Go then and make disciples of all the nations, baptizing them into the name of the Father and of the Son and of the Holy Spirit, 20 Teaching them to observe everything that I have commanded you, and behold, I am with you all the days (perpetually, uniformly, and on every occasion), to the [very] close and consummation of the age. Amen (so let it be).

LUKE 24:44-49 AMPLIFIED BIBLE (AMP)

44 Then He said to them, This is what I told you while I was still with you: everything which is written concerning Me in the Law of Moses and the Prophets and the Psalms must be fulfilled. 45 Then He [thoroughly] opened up their minds to understand the Scriptures, 46 And said to them, Thus it is written that the Christ (the Messiah) should suffer and on the third day rise from (among) the dead, 47 And that repentance [with a view to and as the condition of] forgiveness of sins should be preached in His name to all nations, beginning from Jerusalem. 48 You are witnesses of these things. 49 And behold, I will send forth upon you what My Father has promised; but remain in the city [Jerusalem] until you are clothed with power from on high.

DO THESE SIGNS FOLLOW YOU?

MARK 16:17-18 AMP

17 And these attesting signs will accompany those who believe: in My name they will drive out demons; they will speak in new languages; 18 They will pick up serpents; and [even] if they drink anything deadly, it will not hurt them; they will lay their hands on the sick, and they will get well.

John said we would do greater things than Jesus did. Do you? Are you ready to? Roll up your sleeves because we are stretching out our faith and will practice the Greater works!

JOHN 14:12 AMP

I assure you, most solemnly I tell you, if anyone steadfastly believes in Me, he will himself be able to do the things that I do; and he will do even greater things than these, because I go to the Father.

> *This was written to you. When you hear this, "make disciples of all the nations" and you know He's talking to you, what do you think that means and what will you do about it?*

> *Leader: Consider praying for people or serving someone in your community.*

Doodle Page

KEEP IT SIMPLE— SHARE YOUR STORY

REVELATIONS 12:11 ESV

And they have conquered him by the blood of the Lamb and by the word of their testimony, for they loved not their lives even unto death.

Everyone has a story. Your story describes how Jesus changed your life.

If asked, could you share your story in sixty seconds? Five minutes? Ask God to help you narrow in on your story. Write it down. Practice your story so you will be ready to share it.

> I love how Paul shared his testimony in two short verses in Galatians 1:13-14. In verse 15, however, he basically said, "...but God!" Then Paul spent the rest of Galatians talking about God's grace. In this example, God gets the glory, not Paul's awful, sin-filled past. He spent more time declaring God's redemptive work than on his many past failures.

KEEP YOUR EYES OPEN THIS WEEK FOR OPPORTUNITIES TO SHARE YOUR STORY!

Keep

it

simple.

Period.

Write out your story here.

Remember keep it simple and focused on God's goodness.

Leader: Consider allowing students to share their story with a small group or someone unfamiliar this week.

"BE CAREFUL NOT TO BLAME YOURSELF IF SOMEONE REJECTS CHRIST. IF YOU DO, YOU MIGHT BE TEMPTED TO TAKE CREDIT WHEN SOMEONE ACCEPTS HIM." BRICKS."

— Craig Groeschel

Doodle Page

FAITH WITHOUT WORKS IS DEAD

What good is it to sit in a room worshipping and studying God if we never share it? If you received a new skateboard for Christmas, but you never ride it, isn't that a wasted gift?

Have you ever wasted something you were given?

Sure, there is a time for that. But we MUST get uncomfortable because God gave us the Holy Spirit to comfort us when we are OUT of our comfort territory! This is a great time to learn to rely on Him!

> *"You can't fulfill your calling in your comfort zone!"*
> — STEVEN FURTICK

JAMES 2:14-26

What good is it, my brothers, if someone says he has faith but does not have works? Can that faith save him? 15 If a brother or sister is poorly clothed and lacking in daily food, 16 and one of you says to them, "Go in peace, be warmed and filled," without giving them the things needed for the body, what good[a] is that? 17 So also faith by itself, if it does not have works, is dead.

18 But someone will say, "You have faith and I have works." Show me your faith apart from your works, and I will show you my faith by my works. 19 You believe that God is one; you do well. Even the demons believe—and shudder! 20 Do you want to be shown, you foolish person, that faith apart from works is useless? 21 Was not Abraham our father justified by works when he offered up his son Isaac on the altar? 22 You see that faith was active along with his works, and faith was completed by his works; 23 and the Scripture was fulfilled that says, "Abraham believed God, and it was counted to him as righteousness"—and he was called a friend of God. 24 You see that a person is justified by works and not by faith alone. 25 And in the same way was not also Rahab the prostitute justified by works when she received the messengers and sent them out by another way? 26 For as the body apart from the spirit is dead, so also faith apart from works is dead.

1 CORINTHIANS 4:20

For the kingdom of God does not consist in talk but in power.

> *We plan to pray over your parents. Pray for them now and ask God to give you an encouraging word for them.*

FAITH WITHOUT WORKS IS DEAD

Doodle Page

APPENDIX

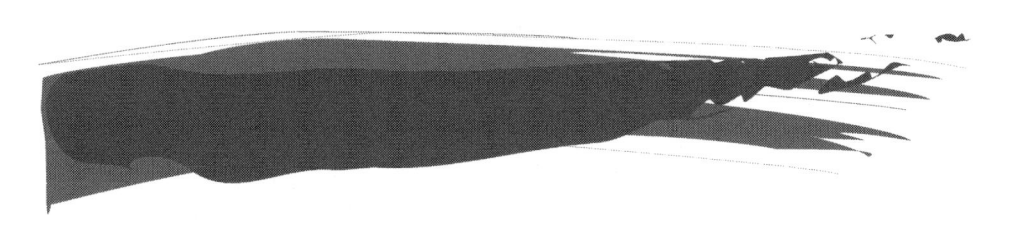

Doodle Page

ISAIAH 43:1-2 ESV

But now thus says the Lord, he who created you, O Jacob, he who formed you, O Israel: "Fear not, for I have redeemed you; I have called you by name, you are mine. When you pass through the waters, I will be with you; and through the rivers, they shall not overwhelm you; when you walk through fire you shall not be burned, and the flame shall not consume you. Isaiah 43:1-2

WHEN JESUS DIDN'T DO MIRACLES

By Ryan Nelson

In the Bible, Jesus performed many miracles. He healed people, held power over nature, and overcame death. But what about the miracles he didn't do? Here are three instances in the Bible where Jesus didn't do the miraculous wonders he was known for:

1. A MIRACLE WITHOUT FAITH

In Mark 6 (and Matthew 13), Jesus returns to Nazareth, his hometown. These people knew Jesus before he started his ministry.

> And on the Sabbath he began to teach in the synagogue, and many who heard him were astonished, saying, "Where did this man get these things? What is the wisdom given to him? How are such mighty works done by his hands? Is not this the carpenter, the son of Mary and brother of James and Joses and Judas and Simon? And are not his sisters here with us?" And they took offense at him (Mark 6:2–3).

Two verses later: "And he could do no mighty work there, except that he laid his hands on a few sick people and healed them" (Mark 6:5). The NLT says, "And because of their unbelief, he couldn't do any miracles among them except to place his hands on a few sick people and heal them."

Whether Jesus couldn't do miracles in Nazareth, or he chose not to, there was no faith, so in this instance, he didn't.

2. A "SIGN FROM HEAVEN"

After Jesus feeds the 4,000 in Decapolis, he and his disciples get into a boat and head to Dalmanutha.

> *The Pharisees came and began to argue with him, seeking from him a sign from heaven to test him. And he sighed deeply in his spirit and said, "Why does this generation seek a sign? Truly, I say to you, no sign will be given to this generation." And he left them, got into the boat again, and went to the other side (Mark 8:11–13).*

Miracles are not for our entertainment. They are not a prerequisite for faith. If all of creation testifies about its creator (Romans 1:20, Psalm 19:1), why should he have to give us a personal sign from heaven on top of that? If you ask God for a sign from heaven like the Pharisees, chances are you'll be disappointed like the Pharisees.

3. A MIRACLE THAT CONTRADICTED GOD'S PLAN

As Jesus hung on the Cross, his divinity was mocked. Again, people wanted to see a sign from heaven, and their requests for a miracle emerged from a severe lack of faith—they did not believe Jesus was who he said he was, and they would not believe him unless the God of the universe did what they asked, right then and there. As he hung there dying, Jesus, who was fully God, could have come down from that cross. Fully man, Jesus may have even been tempted by the prospect (Hebrews 2:18). But he didn't come down.

> *And those who passed by derided him, wagging their heads and saying, "Aha! You who would destroy the temple and rebuild it in three days, save yourself, and come down from the cross!" So also the chief priests with the scribes mocked him to one another, saying, "He saved others; he cannot save himself. Let the Christ, the King of Israel, come down now from the cross that we may see and believe" (Mark 15:29–32).*

APPENDIX

Jesus didn't come down because the Cross had a purpose. The miracle of his survival would have undermined the greater miracle of his resurrection.

It's easy to think about the miracles that Jesus did do. In brief interactions, he radically altered people's lives. But his ways are higher (Isaiah 55:8–9), and because of that, the miracles Jesus didn't do are equally important in helping us understand the inexplicable.

Source: https://blog.faithlife.com/blog/2014/05/3-miracles-jesus-didnt-do/

Doodle Page

YOUR SWORD

MEMORIZE VERSES

This is your sword! Read the Word!

Let's look up some verses and bury them deep in our hearts to stand on later.

Galatians 2:20
John 16:33
Jeremiah 29:11
Romans 2:4
Isaiah 54:17
Isaiah 61
1 John 4:8
1 John 4:4
Ephesians 1:19
Galatians 5:22-23
1 Corinthians 3:16, 6:19
2 Corinthians 6:16
2 Timothy 1:14
Jeremiah 1

Doodle Page

CONFESSIONS

Our words are full of life or death
— you choose.
Confessions help renew your mind
and release life filled words into the
atmosphere.

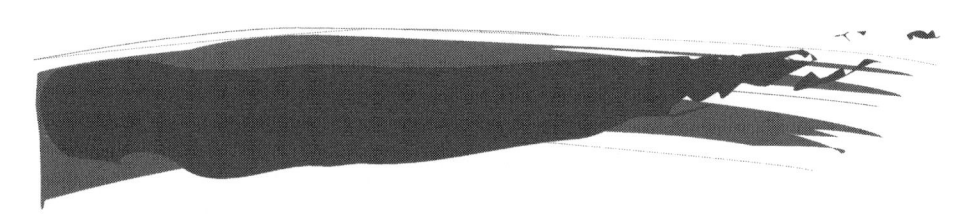

Doodle Page

Even as [in His love] He chose us [actually picked us out for Himself as His own] in Christ before the foundation of the world, that we should be holy (consecrated and set apart for Him) and blameless in His sight, *even* above reproach, before Him in love. Ephesians 1:4 AMP

IDNJC

by Sheri Yates

YOU BELONG TO JESUS.

You are God's child. You belong to Jesus.

YOU ARE CHOSEN BY GOD.

You might not feel special, but God hand-picked you! You know how you shop for the perfect outfit or _____, God specially picked you out!

Synonyms for chosen: selected, special.

YOU ARE GOD'S MASTERPIECE.

This means that you are God's BEST project. It is like an artists finest art project.

Synonyms for masterpiece: work of art, work of genius, stunning success.

YOU ARE FORGIVEN.

Whatever you have done has been paid for – paid in full! There is no sin that wasn't covered by Jesus – One drop of His blood was more than enough to pay for your sin! He carried all your guilt and sin so there is NONE left for you to carry! Stop carrying it! It is not a free license to SIN – it is a free license to live in PEACE!

YOU ARE BLAMELESS.

Have you bee raped, abused, molested, been with a boy – and now you feel like you are tarnished, unclean?

Synonyms for blameless: innocent, spotless, clean, untarnished.

YOU ARE HIS ADOPTED CHILD.

Your parents may be great parents, others – maybe not. Well, if you have ever wished you could belong to a different family – maybe you had wished that your best friends mom could have been your mother. I have good news for you – In Christ, you are adopted into the BEST family EVER! You are God's child now!

Synonyms for adopted: accepted, approved.

YOU ARE PLEASING TO GOD.

Ever felt like you can't do anything right? When God looks at you, He doesn't see all the failures and faults, he looks at you and says "perfect." You are pleasing to Him!

Synonyms for pleasing: pleasant, enjoyable, lovely, gratifying.

YOU ARE SEALED WITH THE HOLY SPIRIT.

You know what that means? It means if you have given your life to Jesus, that you are in Him forever – He will never leave, never forsake, never kick you out of the family, never stop loving you!

WHERE IS MY GOD

by Josh Pugh

He is near the brokenhearted and with the widows and orphans.
He is with the hurting, the sick, the meek, and the pure in heart.
People cry out, and He answers.
People break, and He repairs.
He's the Father of the fatherless, the Protector of the weak.
His children are many, His love unending.
He is at the wall being built, protecting the workers.
The young and the old, He loves all regardless of past or sin.
He is with me, and I am with Him.
He is with the humble.
He is with the sick.
He is with me in the valley of the shadow of death.
He leads me beside still waters.
He is my Shepherd;
He is with His sheep.
He is everywhere.
He comes to the widowed, orphaned, sick, lonely, and weak.
He prepares to save us from Egypt.
He is with us in battle.
He is with us in famine.
My God is always near me and never far.
He is preparing a place for me in His house;
A mansion awaits me.
Here I am in the palm of His hand, loved and cherished.
"Where is my God?" is not the question;
"Where isn't my God?" is.
God is with His people, near the broken, and He sees the hurting.

He is the God of our people.
He is with us and walks before us.
God is in heaven on His throne.
He is always near.
He is with me as a Shepherd, mentor, friend, father, keeper, protector, healer, lover, guide, teacher, but above all these, my Savior.

RELIGION

by Josh Pugh

Lord, let me see You as more than a religion;
Let me see You as more than God.
Let me remember that while I was a sinner, You died for me.
Your love is relentless yet brings peace beyond understanding.
It is shining in us.
Christ redeems us from the curse of the law; therefore, all sickness
and disease, I rebuke you in the name of Jesus.
Any mountain, I rebuke you!
You are to depart my life because my God said, "If you have faith of
a mustard seed, you can say to this mountain, 'Move and be cast in
the sea.'"
We are a people beyond religion; we are kings and priests unto God.
We are more than overcomers: we trample the power of the enemy;
We crush Satan beneath our feet; we trample serpents, scorpions,
and death.
Nothing by any means hurts me.
I am the righteousness of God through Christ.
Nothing will separate me from His love.
I will not fear this war but will praise God amidst the storm.
I will follow God to the land He promised;
He will take me to a land abounding with milk and honey.
I have been given favor.
I am a friend of God.
I'm blessed in coming and in going.
I am above only, not beneath.
I am the head and not the tail.
Like Moses, I will not weaken in sight nor diminish in vigor—

This because the Spirit that raised Christ from the dead lives and dwells in me.
Like Abraham, I will maintain my strength all of my days;
I will spend my years in prosperity and pleasure.
Amen in the name of Jesus!

GOD CHANGES ME

by Josh Pugh

Lord, I meditate on Your Scripture day and night, that I won't sin against You.
I knock; Your Word opens.
I am given Your truth pressed down, shaken together, running over.
God grants me a heart after Him;
He renews my heart and mind.
He loves me!
I'm more than a conqueror.
Through Christ, I overcome by the Blood of the Lamb and the Word of our testimony.
We are inheritors of righteousness.
I resist temptation, and the devil flees from me.
God leads me not into temptation but delivers me from evil.
My help is from the Lord. Freely it was given; freely I receive.
The same Spirit that raised Christ from the dead lives and dwells in me.
He gives me grace for sin, love for hate.
I can do all things through Christ.
I will not fear the pestilence or sudden terror! My help comes from the Lord!
He delivers me and redeems me; He covers me and protects me.
God, You will take my heart of stone and give me a heart of flesh.
I'm no longer broken but am Your workmanship, Your masterpiece.
The work You begin will carry till the day of Christ's redemption.
Day by day, I will not be conformed to this world but changed by the transformation of my mind.
You said, "Be still and know I'm God." Christ is ever renewing my mind. I'm a new creation in Christ.

WHO I AM IN CHRIST

by Josh Pugh

I know now who I am!
I am a child of God.
I am loved and cherished.
No sin separates me from the love of Christ because even when I fall short of God's glory, I am not short of His grace.
Even though I will fail God, He will never fail me.
Even when I lose myself in sin, He will always find me.
He loves me, and I Him.
He is good to me.
He delivers me.
He redeems me.
He freed me and loves me.
I know that He will protect me, care for me, and guide me.
I know, now more than ever: I'm the one Jesus loves!
I am His masterpiece, His lost sheep, His found treasure.
I'm His friend, His child, His ambassador, and His servant.
I am always in His grace, always in His love, never separated from Him.
I am His child.
I am garbed in robes of grace and love, anointed with His love.
I will be radiant with His love.
I will shine with grace and burn with the passion of the One Who frees me from sin and from religion;
He clothes me in light.
I am the righteousness of God through Christ.
I am redeemed.
I am freed.

I am loved, cherished, and ready to show the love I've received.
I'm ready to have faith in Jesus because His love never fails, never gives up, never runs out on me.
I know I am God's workmanship, righteousness, and masterpiece.
I know that if I were the only person on the planet, still God would die for me.
I am redeemed.
When God looks at me, He sees Jesus' perfection because the same Spirit that raised Jesus from the dead is in me.
This is my heritage.
My righteousness is from God.
I am more than a conqueror.
Through Christ, I have conquered tribulation, distress, famine, peril, persecution, the sword, nakedness, weakness, and sin.
I do all of this because of Him Who loves me so.
Who am I?
I am the one God loves.

"THE MINUTE I START BEING AFRAID OF WHAT PEOPLE MIGHT SAY IS THE MINUTE I BECOME USELESS TO GOD."

— Steven Furtick

WHAT AM I

by Josh Pugh

I built my life on things of sand; so when storms hit, it was torn away.
All my life is meaningless without you, God—
Wisdom, treasure, existence itself a burden without Your love.
Your love carries me into the future;
It holds me far from my past.
In my life, where sin once abounded, it is no longer.
You've renewed my heart and mind.
You give me a life for ashes.
You are everlasting, unshakable, Alpha, and Omega.
I was once a slave to sin, but now I serve the Most High.
I was alone, but now I'm constantly in the presence of my King, my God, my Savior.
I'm a companion of angels, an inheritor of blessing.
I give my all to Christ:
I give You all my strength, all my mind, all my soul.
I will seek You all my life.
I am saved by Your Son's death:
While I was a sinner, You died for me;
I am saved, through faith from grace.
It is a gift from You.
As my heart and mind are renewed with each day, I'm thankful knowing that this is from You.
All my days are written in Your book of life.
My name is in that book; and one day, I will see You face to face.
I know I am new because everyone in Christ is a new creation.
Old things pass away;

*All things become new.
I'm an inheritor of righteousness.
I am blessed in coming and in going.
I have been justified through Christ;
My sin was crucified on that cross with my Savior.
He rose from the dead and now lives forever.
Your plans are to prosper me, not to harm me;
They are plans of good and not evil.
Your goodness and blessing overwhelm me daily.
The thief comes to kill, steal, and destroy; but my Savior came to give life, and life abundantly, so young men will dream dreams, old men see visions.
I will speak in tongues of angels because the same Spirit Who raised Christ from the dead lives and dwells in me.
The Word of God does not return void.
There is life and death power in the tongue.
I will only speak life into myself and others because this is what Christ did for me.*

MIND OF CHRIST

by Josh Pugh

You are the head and not the tail,
Above only and not beneath.
You are a tree by rivers of water, whose leaf does not wither.
You prosper and produce your fruit in season.
Like Daniel, you are ten times better in all matters of skill and ability!
You will do good work.
Don't doubt: God reserves the best for His kids.

DEUTERONOMY 28:1-14 ESV

"And if you faithfully obey the voice of the Lord your God, being careful to do all his commandments that I command you today, the Lord your God will set you high above all the nations of the earth. And all these blessings shall come upon you and overtake you, if you obey the voice of the Lord your God. Blessed shall you be in the city, and blessed shall you be in the field. Blessed shall be the fruit of your womb and the fruit of your ground and the fruit of your cattle, the increase of your herds and the young of your flock. Blessed shall be your basket and your kneading bowl. Blessed shall you be when you come in, and blessed shall you be when you go out. "The Lord will cause your enemies who rise against you to be defeated before you. They shall come out against you one way and flee before you seven ways. The Lord will command the blessing on you in your barns and in all that you undertake. And he will bless you in the land that the Lord your God is giving you. The Lord will establish you as a people holy to himself, as he has sworn to you, if you keep the commandments of the Lord your God and walk in his ways. And all the peoples of the earth shall see that you are called by the name of the Lord,

and they shall be afraid of you. And the Lord will make you abound in prosperity, in the fruit of your womb and in the fruit of your livestock and in the fruit of your ground, within the land that the Lord swore to your fathers to give you. The Lord will open to you his good treasury, the heavens, to give the rain to your land in its season and to bless all the work of your hands. And you shall lend to many nations, but you shall not borrow. And the Lord will make you the head and not the tail, and you shall only go up and not down, if you obey the commandments of the Lord your God, which I command you today, being careful to do them, and if you do not turn aside from any of the words that I command you today, to the right hand or to the left, to go after other gods to serve them.

LEADER

PRACTICE OPPORTUNITIES

Faith without works is dead. The following include some opportunities to hear from God, practice, minister to those in your youth group, your families, and even complete strangers.

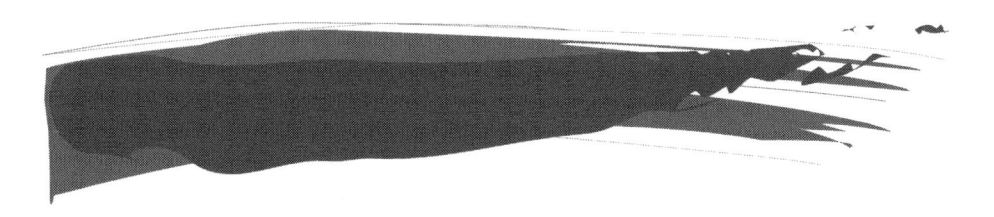

Doodle Page

ONE WORD

HEBREWS 3:13 AMP

But instead warn (admonish, urge, and encourage) one another every day, as long as it is called Today, that none of you may be hardened [into settled rebellion] by the deceitfulness of sin [by the fraudulence, the stratagem, the trickery which the delusive glamor of his sin may play on him].

Today we will huddle in a circle.

Half the group will sit. The other half will stand behind someone.

The standing student: Pray and ask God for a Word – just one Word to speak or pray over the person in front of you.

Remain in worship as you allow God's words to minister to the student.

Switch seats.

Once complete, move of with the remainder of the group.

SPEAK A BLESSING

Search through your notes in this book or scripture to find a blessing to speak and pray over the person assigned to you.

When you are not sure what to speak and pray, consider some of the following:

- ✓ Protection from the evil one – Psalm 91
- ✓ God's blessing from Deuteronomy – 28:1-14
- ✓ To know God more intimately – Ephesians 1:17-21
- ✓ I am charts from above

HOMETOWN MISSIONARY FORM

Your Life as a Mission Trip is to pray in advance and ask God who you are looking for. This is an easy start, but then it will become a lifestyle.

1. Pray and complete the chart below.
2. Form groups of three or four.
    - Combine group lists on the right.
    - Each member hold your own list
3. Choose your location – the grocery store, park, skating?
4. Start looking for people to pray for.
5. When someone matches your list, approach slowly with respect and honor…
    - Say something like: "This may seem a little odd, but we prayed and ask God who we should pray for and we think you're on our list."
    - Show them your list. (They may see themselves on your list.)
    - Build rapport. (Ask questions to get to know them.)
    - Let them know God has highlighted them, and wants to bless them.
    - Ask if you can pray for them. '

6. If they say "No" – Bless them and move to the next opportunity.
7. If they say "Yes'" Pray. Ask if you can set your hand on them. Only touch above the shoulders.
8. Ask them if they would like to have a relationship with Jesus personally.
   - Help them ask Jesus into their life.
   - Jesus, I know that I have sinned against you. Thank you for forgiving me of my sins. I believe that you are the Son of God and the only way to the Father. I receive you as my personal Lord and Savior. Holy Spirit fill me now and continue this good work that you have started in me.
   - If someone is not on your list, but is clearly in need of prayer, don't pass up the opportunity.

Pray and Write down anything you hear in the space below.

Location (stop sign, bench digital clock, coffee shop, Target, Wal-Mart, etc.)

_____   _____   _____   _____

_____   _____   _____   _____

Person's name or appearance

_____   _____   _____   _____

_____   _____   _____   _____

What might they need prayer for (knee brace, cane, kidneys, tumor, left ankle, marriage, etc.)

_____   _____   _____   _____

_____   _____   _____   _____

The unusual (lollipop, windmill, lime-green door, dolphins, etc.)

_____   _____   _____   _____

_____   _____   _____   _____

LISTENING

PSALM 46:10 AMP

Let be and be still, and know (recognize and understand) that I am God. I will be exalted among the nations! I will be exalted in the earth.

Listen to the worship music and write down below all the words that strike you. Continue listening. Now, write down why these words struck you. Consider drawing a picture, poem, spoken word, prayer, or song to describe it.

SPEAK LIFE

ROMANS 12:2 AMP

Do not be conformed to this world (this age), [fashioned after and adapted to its external, superficial customs], but be transformed (changed) by the [entire] renewal of your mind [by its new ideals and its new attitude], so that you may prove [for yourselves] what is the good and acceptable and perfect will of God, even the thing which is good and acceptable and perfect [in His sight for you].

Use the I am statements for this.

Youth hold hands with the same gender person in your group. Look each other in the eyes while you listen to some verses or the I Am statements.

Fully receive these words as you hear them.

Leader will read these statements over the youth. Ask one of them to repeat you – one at a time – to the person they are holding hands with.

Hopefully, everyone's identity is strengthened from listening.

SEARCH FOR JESUS IN OTHERS

The I AM statements will be helpful here.

Leader will read these statements to the youth.

The youth should hold hands and look each other in the eyes while the leader reads some verses or the I Am statements.

Students should look deep into the other student's eyes to search for Jesus within them. Your vision of the person's hands you are holding should change as Christ is revealed in their eyes.

Ask them to hold their stare for five minutes. It's uncomfortable. Look through the eyes into the heart.

Pray over one another.

SERVE

GALATIANS 5:13 AMP

For you, brethren, were [indeed] called to freedom; only [do not let your] freedom be an incentive to your flesh and an opportunity or excuse [for [a]selfishness], but through love you should serve one another.

Find a place to serve. Does your church have a place you can serve behind the scenes or a place you can minister to others?

Consider serving together regularly so that they can connect and build unity through experiences outside your youth group meeting time.

Use all the gifts. Take all that you have learned here and go out to change atmospheres and bring life every place you step! This is the perfect place to maintain your attitude of acquisition.

WASH FEET

JOHN 13:8 AMP

Peter said to Him, You shall never wash my feet! Jesus answered him, Unless I wash you, you have no part with (in) Me [you have no share in companionship with Me]."

Leaders, wash some of the youth's feet to model Jesus servant life.

Next, have the youth wash each other's feet. Consider maintaining gender separation.

Discuss how it felt to wash someone else's feet and how it felt to have your own feet washed.

- Were your feet clean or dirty?
- Were you ashamed?
- Did you feel like you should be helping?
- Did you feel guilty?
- Did you enjoy serving or was it a burden?
- How were the feet of those you washed? Clean or dirty? Stinky or fresh?

Listen to the story of Jesus washing the feet of His disciples. Turn on some worship and give the students an opportunity to praise God for all that He did.

*Consider writing down all the student's emotions and comments about this practice opportunity. Post it on the wall so they can see it.

We met a man from iHOP that switched shirts with a homeless man. The homeless man told him how much he loved the iHOP guy's shirt so he said, "I will give it to you, but I don't have another shirt. Do you want to trade shirts with me?" The homeless guy jumped on the opportunity to have a new shirt.

Most of you are probably like me...."eeeeeewww!" ikr!!

BUT!!!!

It is the most simple gospel message, right?! It is a perfect representation of the GOOD NEWS!

Why do you think so? Because....Jesus took our stanky rags and traded them for new clean ones!

I am confident that will never be forgotten by the homeless man! Remember that while you think this is nasty, it is exactly what Jesus did for you!

ORIGINAL DESIGN PRAYER

JEREMIAH 1:5 AMP

Before I formed you in the womb I knew [and] approved of you [as My chosen instrument], and before you were born I separated and set you apart, consecrating you; [and] I appointed you as a prophet to the nations.

The leader will pray over you one-on-one. They will ask God to give them words that God has for you. Those words should encourage you or be confirmation of something God has already spoken to you.

Take notes or audio record each prayer because sometimes, you will love having this to encourage you when trouble comes.

The student should practice hearing from the Lord too. Don't make it up. Ask Father for a Word that only that person would know. If the student hears a Word, be encouraged to speak it aloud.

This will increase boldness with men and build confidence in hearing God's voice.

It's completely acceptable to read a verse, etc. over them.

- ✓ Select the first student
- ✓ Pray

- ✓ Listen
- ✓ If you hear from the Lord, share it.
- ✓ Record or write it down.

Consider inviting parents or friends of the group in to have the youth pray their original design over them.

Doodles and Notes

"PRAYER MEANS THAT WE HAVE COME BOLDLY INTO THE THRONE ROOM AND WE ARE STANDING IN GOD'S PRESENCE."

—E. W. Kenyon

Doodles and Notes

"FAITH TALKS IN THE LANGUAGE OF GOD. DOUBT TALKS IN THE LANGUAGE OF MAN."

—E. W. Kenyon

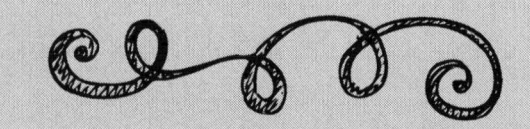

Doodles and Notes

"WE HAVE BEEN CREATED FOR GOD AND BY GOD TO TRANSFORM THE WORLD AROUND US."

— Christine Caine

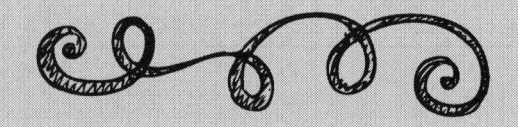

Doodles and Notes

"YOU CANNOT HAVE A POSITIVE LIFE AND A NEGATIVE MIND."

— Joyce Meyer

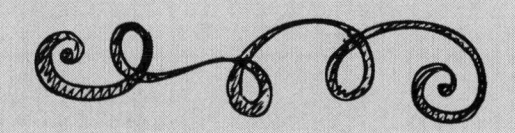

ACKNOWLEDGEMENTS

Thank you to <u>Steal like an Artist</u> by Austin Kleon. You inspired me! If I hadn't had read your book, I am not sure that I could have pulled off this project. Thank you for paving the way ahead of me and for being a pioneer.

Thank you to Kathleen for dreamstorming about taking the Original Design Youth deeper.

Thank you Kathleen, Taylor, Jaden, Hannah, and Emily for leading the youth of iKan Ministries into the depths of God's presence. Thank you for your faithfulness week after week. Thank you for helping the youth encounter God's love while learning to respond in worship.

Thank you Katie Candle Moore and Spencer Lauren Yates for your artistic skills by providing all the images for this book.

Josh, your anointed words will surely bless many Youths and families for years to come. Thank you for allowing us to use them freely. I love your right to copy policy – "please do." We love you so much! Your prayers and Hannah's continue carrying an atmosphere of change and power at Avodah and across our city!

Thank you to Nona for working around the clock to help me get this project pounded out. I appreciate you so much. You are my right hand.

Thank you to Jesus who laid down his life for me and for all of us so we could truly be free.

Thank you to iKan Ministries and Avodah for providing space for worshipful atmosphere and around the clock worship over our city and state.

Thank you to SOAR Bible Study, soarwithgod.com for some of the content, which I nabbed from our Bible study, Amy! We always dreamed of seeing SOAR for Youth…maybe someday. I pray this will have a similar impact as SOAR!

Ty, goodness. Thank you for tolerating my absence while I plunged forward with my head down and pencil up! Thank you for speaking truth in love so that I would not become entangled in opportunities to be offended this week otherwise I would have been distracted and missed this amazing work of God. I love you.

Spencer, Chandler, and Kennedi—oh, how I love you so. I am sorry that I have been absent this week. I assure you that I have laid out something planned by God to bless your foundation in Him for future generations. I love you and pray that this will help you encounter the love of the Father! I love, love, love you! Honored to be your mom!

"I MAY NOT BE WHERE I WANT TO BE, BUT THANK GOD I AM NOT WHERE I USED TO BE."

— Joyce Meyer

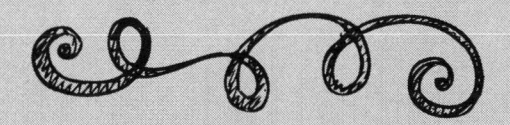

Doodle Page

ABOUT THE BOOK, AUTHOR, AND DIRECTOR OF G.O.D.

DISCOVER G.O.D.
— GOD'S ORIGINAL DESIGN for YOUTH

Looking for a youth group that calls your inner Jesus freak to a higher standard? Welcome to Original Design! We do not look down on youth, but rather look to them to be the right generation to know God and make Him known around the world! This is not your afterschool childcare kind of youth experience. Rather, we dig into God's word. We explore who they are in Christ and ask them to walk it out with challenges and mission work in their own home! Sounds better than grandma's biscuits – because it is! Ages 12-18 are welcome on Wednesdays to dive in deeper with us!. Learn more: youth@ikanministries.com. Also find us at www.ikanminsistries.com.

Sheri Yates is a Pastor and the President of iKAN Ministries where we love God and others to influence nations to love God and love others!

Kathleen Hildenbrand, Pastor at iKAN Ministries and Original Design. Newlywed, married to Taylor. She loves the Lord and loves these youth. She leads her team diligently. She prays over the youth and their families faithfully. Kathleen co-labored on the origination of Truth or Trash and was instrumental in the start up of iKAN and the Avodah Prayer Room. She mans our 24 hour prayer line where she encourages many from around the nation in Truth, love, and prayer. Sheri and Kathleen are sisters and Dreamstorm partners for O.D. and this book.

We desire to take these students, who have such limitless potential, more into the presence and power of God. We can see how lies try to slip in and the thief tries to steal, but we are confident in the Lord's promises and that He always redeems what the locusts attempt to destroy!

We pray that this book is used by many and will change the world through these awesome young adults who chase after God's heart.

Made in the USA
Columbia, SC
15 April 2017